Voices of the American Revolution
in the Carolinas

OTHER TITLES IN THE REAL VOICES, REAL HISTORY™ SERIES

The Jamestown Adventure: Accounts of the Virginia Colony, 1605–1614, edited by Ed Southern

Hark the Sound of Tar Heel Voices: 220 Years of UNC History, edited by Daniel W. Barefoot

Voices from St. Simons: Personal Narratives of an Island's Past, edited by Stephen Doster

Cherokee Voices: Early Accounts of Cherokee Life in the East, edited by Vicki Rozema

Voices from the Trail of Tears, edited by Vicki Rozema

Far More Terrible for Women: Personal Accounts of Women in Slavery, edited by Patrick Minges

Black Indian Slave Narratives, edited by Patrick Minges

No Man's Yoke on My Shoulders: Personal Accounts of Slavery in Florida, edited by Horace Randall Williams

Weren't No Good Times: Personal Accounts of Slavery in Alabama, edited by Horace Randall Williams

I Was Born in Slavery: Personal Accounts of Slavery in Texas, edited by Andrew Waters

Prayin' to Be Set Free: Personal Accounts of Slavery in Mississippi, edited by Andrew Waters

On Jordan's Stormy Banks: Personal Accounts of Slavery in Georgia, edited by Andrew Waters

Mighty Rough Times, I Tell You: Personal Accounts of Slavery in Tennessee, edited by Andrea Sutcliffe

My Folks Don't Want Me to Talk About Slavery: Personal Accounts of Slavery in North Carolina, edited by Belinda Hurmence

Before Freedom, When I Just Can Remember: Personal Accounts of Slavery in South Carolina, edited by Belinda Hurmence

We Lived in a Little Cabin in the Yard: Personal Accounts of Slavery in Virginia, edited by Belinda Hurmence

Voices of the American Revolution
in the Carolinas

EDITED BY ED SOUTHERN

JOHN F. BLAIR
PUBLISHER   Winston-Salem, North Carolina

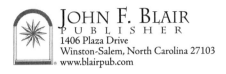

JOHN F. BLAIR
PUBLISHER
1406 Plaza Drive
Winston-Salem, North Carolina 27103
www.blairpub.com

Manufactured in the United States of America

COVER ILLUSTRATION
The Battle of Kings Mountain
Painting by Don Troiani, www.historicalimagebank.com

BOOK DESIGN BY DEBRA LONG HAMPTON

Library of Congress Cataloging-in-Publication Data
Voices of the American Revolution in the Carolinas / edited by Ed Southern.
p.   cm.   —   (Real voices, real history series)
Includes bibliographical references.
ISBN 978-0-89587-358-3 (alk. paper)
1.   North Carolina—History—Revolution, 1775–1783—Personal narratives.
2.   South Carolina—History—Revolution, 1775–1783—Personal narratives.
3.   United States—History—Revolution, 1775–1783—Personal narratives.
4.   United States. Continental Army—Biography.   5.   Great Britain. Army—Biography.   I.   Southern, Ed, 1972–
E275.A2V65 2009
973.3'4560922—dc22
          2008044757

Contents

Introduction ix
Timeline of Events...xviii

Part I: "Times Began to Be Troublesome,"
1775–1776

The Meck Dec, from the *Southern Literary Messenger* 3

Persuading the Back Country, by William Henry Drayton
and the Reverend William Tennent..16

The Making of a Tory Partisan, from *The Narrative of
Colonel David Fanning*... 28

Account of the Attack on Fort Moultrie, from
the *South Carolina and American General Gazette*
of August 2, 1776 37

Part II: Cornwallis Comes to Carolina,
January–August 1780

The Siege of Charleston, from *Memoirs of the
American Revolution*, by General William Moultrie 53

Buford's Quarter, from *A History of the Campaigns of 1780 and 1781 in the Southern Provinces of North America*, by Banastre Tarleton..65

Moffitt's Minute Men, from *Autobiography of a Revolutionary Soldier*, by James Collins................................73

The Battle of Ramsour's Mill, from *The Revolutionary War Sketches of William R. Davie* 80

The Battle at Stallions, from *The Memoir of Major Thomas Young* 86

Huck's Defeat, from *Colonel William Hill's Memoirs of the Revolution* 89

The Gamecock, from *Colonel William Hill's Memoirs of the Revolution* 95

A Narrative of the Battle of Camden, from "A Narrative of the Campaign of 1780," by Colonel Otho Holland Williams 101

Part III: The Partisans Rise,
September–October 1780

The Swamp Fox, from *The Life of General Francis Marion*, by Brigadier General Peter Horry and Parson M. L. Weems.. 119

The Hornet's Nest, from *The Revolutionary War Sketches of William R. Davie* and from *A History of the Campaigns of 1780 and 1781 in the Southern Provinces of North America*, by Banastre Tarleton 127

Aunt Susie and Andy Jackson, by Dr. John H. Gibbon, in a letter to the *National Intelligencer*, August 29, 1845 136

Fanning's "Rules and Regulations," from *The Narrative of Colonel David Fanning* 143

Part IV: "Lay Waste with Fire and Sword,"
October 1780–January 1781

Kings Mountain, from a pamphlet by Isaac Shelby; from *Autobiography of a Revolutionary Soldier*, by James Collins; and from *The Memoir of Major Thomas Young* 151

The Battle of the Cowpens, from General Daniel Morgan's report to Nathanael Greene and from *The Memoir of Major Thomas Young* 171

Part V: "Then He Is Ours,"
February–March 1781

The Battle of Cowan's Ford, from *Narrative of the Battle of Cowan's Ford*, by Robert Henry 191

The Race to the Dan, from *Memoirs of the War in the Southern Department of the United States* by General Henry "Light Horse Harry" Lee 200

The Battle of Guilford Courthouse, from *Memoirs of the War in the Southern Department of the United States* by General Henry "Light Horse Harry" Lee 219

Part VI: Endgame,
September 1781–December 1782

The Battle of Eutaw Springs, by Nathanael Greene, in a letter to Congress 235

A Loyalist Seeks Refuge, from *The Narrative of Colonel David Fanning* 243

Bibliography 250

Introduction

"Allow what you will for esprit de corps, for this or for that, the thing that sent him swinging up the slope ... was nothing more or less than his conviction, the conviction of every farmer among what was essentially only a band of farmers, that nothing living could cross him and get away with it."

W. J. Cash,
The Mind of the South

"There's no such thing as tough. There's trained and untrained."

Denzel Washington,
Man on Fire

On February 11, 1780, a British army led by General Sir Henry Clinton came ashore on Johns Island, South Carolina, and brought the full force of the American Revolution into the Carolinas. By the end of March, the British laid siege to Charleston, South Carolina's capital and the most important city south of Philadelphia. By the middle of May, they had taken the city and the American army defending it.

On March 15, 1781, that same British army left the field at Guilford Courthouse exhausted, decimated, stripped of supplies and rations, and victorious in name only. Its march away from Guilford Courthouse would end only a few months later at Yorktown, Virginia, where the British would be the besieged and would be the ones to surrender.

A year that began with the British sweeping aside all opposition, capturing the only other army in the Carolinas worthy of the name, and marching victorious through the gates of the region's only true city ended with them limping almost 200 miles through the back country to the loyal port of Wilmington, desperate for resupply, harried by partisans, plagued by desertion, and knowing that they were—as their opponent at Guilford Courthouse had said—"ruined" as an effective force.[1]

How did this happen? How did 13 months in the Carolinas bring the mighty redcoats so low that George Washington's Continental Army—after six years of barely hanging in against its foe, with considerable help from the French—was able to contain them and successfully demand their surrender just a few months later? What were the factors that caused this reversal of fortune? And what did it feel like to be part of this "history of miracles"?[2]

Historians have debated the causes for more than two centuries: the British were too arrogant; they were too aggressive; they reached too far and spread their supply line too thin; they underestimated Nathanael Greene and Daniel Morgan; they overestimated their loyalist support; and, not to be overlooked, they made the still-often-fatal mistake of personally insulting a bunch of rednecks.

Historians have too often ignored, though, the other way of answering how the British army came to ruin: how it felt to live, fight, and try to survive the American Revolution in the Carolinas. What was it like to be British or American, Tory or Whig, regular soldier or militia, partisan or outlaw or would-be bystander as the two sides (and those who drifted from side to side) went at each other with a fury across the Carolina countryside?

Voices of the American Revolution in the Carolinas largely leaves the causes to other writers and looks at how the war felt, through eyewitness accounts of those who fought the battles and skirmishes.

Colonial Carolinians

Most Americans believe only one civil war has been fought on United States soil. In the Carolinas, though, the American Revolution was as much a war of neighbor against neighbor as a war of independence. Until the very end, the population was split between those who saw patriotism as devotion to American liberty and those who saw patriotism as devotion to the established British rule under which they had always lived.

Between these two committed extremes, the people were further split into those who wished only for peace and stability, whether supplied by an American or British government, and those who took advantage of the violence and chaos of the war to prey on those around them.

In 1776, about 150,000 people lived in the colonies of North and South Carolina. Though geographically smaller, South Carolina was by far the more prosperous. In fact, it was the richest of all the 13 American colonies.[3] Its capital, Charleston, was the third-largest city in the colonies, behind only New York and Philadelphia. Settled in 1670 by 148 mostly English men and women, Charleston by 1770 had become the most important port south of Philadelphia and the richest city in North America, the town and the surrounding Low Country home to an estimated 88,244 settlers, 19,066 of them white and 69,178 black.[4] Though the majority of the colony's white citizens lived in the back country, its government was dominated by the "rice kings," the Low Country planters who made their fortunes through the cultivation of rice. For the most part, the plantations occupied a narrow strip of land between the Savannah River and Winyah Bay; the rice kings lived either on those plantations or in Charleston.

Though North Carolina had been the site of England's first attempt to colonize North America—the ill-fated Lost Colony of Roanoke Island, which landed in 1587—it was by and large one of the poorest and least-settled of the original 13 colonies. Its largest town was Wilmington, a river port eclipsed by the larger harbors of Charleston and the Chesapeake Bay. Much of eastern North Carolina's population had drifted south from the Virginia Tidewater. Though that population included a significant share of wealthy planters, their numbers and affluence did not compare to that of the South Carolina Low Country.

The back country of both Carolinas—usually defined as beginning 50 miles inland from the Atlantic coast and reaching to or beyond the Blue Ridge Mountains—had been the scene of an immigrant influx to rival the later immigration waves of the 19th century. More than 100,000 European settlers moved into the Carolina back country between 1700 and 1776, most of them arriving during the decade prior to independence. Some came inland from the Carolina coastal plain, but most traveled south along the Great Wagon Road from Virginia, Maryland, or Pennsylvania. They or their parents were English, German, French Huguenot, Swiss, Welsh, or—most numerously—British Borderers, the cultural group usually lumped together as Scots-Irish. While many were truly Scots-Irish (lowland Scots transplanted to Ulster), the Borderers included lowland Scots come directly from Scotland and English from Yorkshire, Northumberland, Cumberland, and other counties along the Scottish border. They were the dominant cultural group of the Carolina back country, and they brought with them a long heritage of pride and clannishness, developed over centuries in a contested and often lawless frontier that was the site of nearly constant invasions, wars, feuds, and banditry on both large and small scales.[5]

First in Freedom

These Carolinians did not stand up as one for liberty after

the Revolutionary War commenced at Lexington and Concord (Massachusetts, not North Carolina) in 1775, nor after the signing of the Declaration of Independence in 1776. The majority were, in all likelihood, ambivalent at best about being citizens of a new nation. More than a few were not happy about it at all.

The seeds of independence, however, had been planted years before in the Carolinas, and they would bear early fruit. The Regulator movement is subject enough for a book of its own; the streamlined version of the story is that back-country farmers rose up against the royal government and the coastal-plain planters who dominated it. Tired of the combination of high taxes and little or no law enforcement or government service, they banded together as "Regulators" to regulate their own affairs. The Regulators attacked county courts and officials and, in North Carolina, threatened the colonial assembly in New Bern. In response, Royal Governor William Tryon called out the militia and crushed the Regulators at the Battle of Alamance Creek in 1771.[6] Although the Regulator movement failed, many in the back country gained valuable experience in self-organization and partisan warfare. More than that, a precedent had been set: among the Regulators' rallying cries was "No taxation without representation."[7]

Tryon's successor as royal governor was Josiah Martin, described by North Carolina historian William S. Powell as "suddenly in a position that required almost every intellectual quality which he lacked."[8] His attempts to prevent North Carolina delegates from attending the first Continental Congress in 1774 were circumvented by John Harvey, the speaker of the assembly, who organized a provincial assembly without the governor's approval, proving to Martin—and, more importantly, to North Carolinians—that they were quite capable of governing themselves. Martin also provoked 51 women in and around Edenton to convene a "tea party," at which they pledged to support the American cause against British tyranny.

At the same time, the rice kings were watching Britain's response to the Massachusetts uprising with grave concern. If the British could close the port of Boston, they could surely do the same to Charleston. The rice kings already knew they were capable of governing themselves and anyone else in their domain. By 1775, they established their own provincial congress without royal authorization. As the fighting in the Northeast continued to escalate, the new Whig governments of both states began to take steps to defend themselves, seizing arsenals and expanding their militias.

Voices of the Revolution

The accounts in this volume are taken from first-person narratives by those who served in the American Revolution in the Carolinas, from officers such as Henry "Light Horse Harry" Lee and Banastre Tarleton to teenage scouts such as Thomas Young and James Collins. Some accounts, like Daniel Morgan's report of the Battle of the Cowpens, were written immediately or soon after the action; others, like Young's, were written when the boy soldiers had become old men. Some were written (and sometimes embellished) specifically for publication, while others were written as private correspondence or official reports. Some express a great deal of emotion and describe only the authors' immediate experiences of war, while others concentrate on logistics, strategy, tactics, and the practical realities of an army in battle; some, like Lee's, manage to do both.

I selected these accounts to give as full a portrait of the Revolutionary War in the Carolinas as the format of the Real Voices, Real History™ series would allow. Although I often applied modern rules of spelling and punctuation to the accounts, I left the authors' grammar and construction as written. I also left alone the curious 18th-century habit of some authors to refer to themselves in the third person, which I hope will not cause confusion.

Those who fought for the American cause in the War of Independence have been mythologized over the last two centuries into upright, stout-hearted men, pure in their motives, dedication, and courage. The reality of those who fight any war is far more messy, more fascinating, and more deserving of attention and sympathy. The American Revolution in the Carolinas was nasty, brutish, and relatively short, though it must not have felt short to those who lived through it. It moved with a furious swiftness, the center of action shifting from Charleston to Camden, from Charlotte to Kings Mountain, from the Cowpens to Guilford Courthouse in a matter of months, weeks, or sometimes days. I hope the accounts in *Voices of the American Revolution in the Carolinas* give some idea of what it was like to be part of that war, when two states were ripped apart but a nation was made.

Notes

[1] John Buchanan, *The Road to Guilford Courthouse: The American Revolution in the Carolinas* (New York: John Wiley & Sons, 1997), 382.

[2] Peter Horry and M. L. Weems, *The Life of General Francis Marion* (Winston-Salem, N.C.: John F. Blair, Publisher, 2000), 105.

[3] Walter Edgar, *Partisans and Redcoats: The Southern Conflict That Turned the Tide of the American Revolution* (New York: Harper Perennial, 2003), xi.

[4] Buchanan, *The Road to Guilford Courthouse*, 22.

[5] David Hackett Fischer, *Albion's Seed: Four British Folkways in America* (New York: Oxford University Press, 1989), 621–32.

[6] William S. Powell, *North Carolina: A History* (Chapel Hill: University of North Carolina Press, 1988), 49–50.

[7] John S. Pancake, *This Destructive War: The British Campaign in the Carolinas, 1780–1782* (Tuscaloosa: University of Alabama Press, 1985), 21.

[8] Powell, *North Carolina*, 56.

Timeline of Events

1775

<u>May 20</u>
Whigs in Mecklenburg County, North Carolina, approve the Mecklenburg Declaration of Independence.

<u>August–September</u>
William Tennent, William Henry Drayton, and others tour the South Carolina back country espousing the cause of liberty.

<u>November 19</u>
The Tories, including David Fanning, attack the rebel fort at Ninety-Six, South Carolina.

<u>December</u>
Rebels under Colonel Richard Richardson wage the successful Snow Campaign against Tories in upstate South Carolina.

1776

<u>February 27</u>
North Carolina militia under Colonels Richard Caswell and Alexander Lillington defeat loyalist Highlanders at the Battle of Moores Creek Bridge.

June 28
South Carolina troops under William Moultrie turn back
a British invasion fleet at the Battle of Sullivan's Island,
preventing the first British attack on Charleston.

July–October
The Cherokees, on the side of the loyalists, attack Whig
settlements in the back country of South Carolina.

1778

December 29
Savannah, Georgia, falls to the British.

1780

February 11
British troops under General Sir Henry Clinton (with
Charles, Lord Cornwallis, as second-in-command) land
on the South Carolina coast and begin their march to
Charleston.

March 29
Clinton's army lays siege to Charleston.

May 12
Charleston surrenders to Clinton.

<u>May 29</u>
Lieutenant Colonel Banastre Tarleton's British Legion massacres surrendered Continental soldiers under Abraham Buford in the Waxhaws near the North Carolina–South Carolina border. This gives rise to the rebel rallying cry of "Buford's Quarter," as well as to Tarleton nicknames such as "Bloody Ban" and "Ban the Butcher."

<u>June 18</u>
Captain Christian Huck burns Colonel William Hill's ironworks in the South Carolina back country.

<u>June 20</u>
Rebel militia, though outnumbered, attack and scatter an encampment of Tory partisans at the Battle of Ramsour's Mill.

<u>July 12</u>
The Battles of Huck's Defeat and Stallions in the South Carolina back country are both victories for rebel partisans.

<u>August 1</u>
General Thomas Sumter leads his rebel partisans to a victory at Hanging Rock and a stalemate at Rocky Mount, both in South Carolina. Among the rebel participants in these actions are Colonel William Hill, Colonel William Richardson Davie, and Davie's young scout, Andrew Jackson.

<u>August 6</u>
Rebel partisans win the second battle at Hanging Rock.

August 16
The British under Lord Cornwallis rout the Continentals and rebel militia under General Horatio Gates at Camden, South Carolina.

Late August
Rebel partisans under Colonel (later General) Francis Marion attack a column of British troops escorting prisoners from Camden to Charleston. In the coming months, Marion will harass the British and Tories continually and earn his legend as "the Swamp Fox."

September 26
British troops under Cornwallis capture Charlotte after facing effective, though outmatched, resistance from local rebels led by William Richardson Davie. Cornwallis establishes a headquarters at Charlotte, but the surrounding countryside remains so hostile that he calls Mecklenburg County "a damn'd hornet's nest of rebellion."

October 7
Rebel militia and partisans, including the Overmountain Men from the Watauga settlements, defeat Tory troops under Patrick Ferguson at the Battle of Kings Mountain.

October 14
Cornwallis pulls his army out of Charlotte to create a winter camp at Winnsboro, South Carolina.

December 2
Nathanael Greene arrives in Charlotte to take command of

the Southern Department of the Continental Army from
Horatio Gates.

December 16
Greene moves the bulk of his army from depleted Charlotte
to Cheraw, South Carolina, while sending Daniel Morgan
with a light corps of about 600 men west of the Catawba
River.

1781

January 16
Continental troops and rebel militia under Daniel Morgan
defeat Tarleton's British Legion at the Battle of the Cowpens,
the first rebel victory over regular British troops in a formal
battle in the South.

January 19
Cornwallis breaks winter camp to pursue Morgan's light
corps into North Carolina.

February 1
Having burned his army's baggage at Ramsour's Mill to travel
more swiftly, Cornwallis crosses the Catawba River with his
troops while under fire from rebel militia and partisans in the
Battle of Cowan's Ford.

February–March
The armies of Cornwallis and Greene compete in the Race to
the Dan. Cornwallis hopes to catch Greene before he can get

his army to safety in Virginia, on the north side of the Dan River, so as to force him into a final, conclusive fight.

March 15
Regrouped Continentals and rebel militia under Greene face British troops under Cornwallis at the Battle of Guilford Courthouse. Though the British claim a technical victory because Greene leaves the field, their army in the South is left a shadow of its former self.

September 8
British troops defeat Greene's Continentals and militia at the Battle of Eutaw Springs in South Carolina, but the victory ruins the British army in the Carolinas, making it unfit for further fighting. Eutaw Spring is the final major Revolutionary War battle in the Carolinas.

October 19
Cornwallis surrenders at Yorktown.

1782

December 14
British forces evacuate Charleston, prompting a massive emigration of loyalists to Canada and British Florida.

PART I

"Times Began to be Troublesome"
1775–1776

The Meck Dec

From the *Southern Literary Messenger*[1]

On May 20, 1775, citizens in Mecklenburg County, North Carolina, were the first in what would become the United States to call for independence from Great Britain.

Maybe.

Without question, some of Mecklenburg's leading citizens met on May 19 to discuss the volatile political situation in the colonies, particularly Massachusetts, and what they should do about it. Without question, many of those same citizens met two weeks later, on May 31, and produced at that meeting the Mecklenburg Resolves, protesting Great Britain's abrogations of the colonists' rights but stopping just short of calling for independence.

What remains a question is whether or not those citizens, as their May 19 meeting stretched into the next day, composed and signed their names to a document known as the Mecklenburg Declaration of Independence, or "Meck Dec" for short. The signers dispatched Captain James Jack to Philadelphia to present the Continental Congress with a copy of their declaration, but the Congress refused to recognize such an inflammatory document, and no record of its presentation was entered into the congressional minutes.

If such an inflammatory document was produced in the first place, of course.

The Meck Dec was largely forgotten outside the Carolinas until June 5, 1819, when the Essex Register of Salem, Massachusetts, reprinted a Raleigh newspaper's story about the declaration, along with a text reconstructed from participants' memories. A few weeks later, John Adams sent his friend Thomas Jefferson a copy of the article, praising the Meck Dec signers and noting the similarities between the language of the Meck Dec and that of Jefferson's national Declaration of Independence. The Founding Father and third president of the United States responded with what can best be described as a snit, saying he had never heard of the Mecklenburg declaration, and that it was probably a fake. Several newspapers published Jefferson's letter, and the fight was on. The state of North Carolina commissioned a special study to determine (i.e., prove) the Meck Dec's authenticity. Scholars, archivists, children of the Meck Dec signers, and bystanders with nothing better to do weighed in.

The debate got ugly in 1837 when George Tucker, Jefferson's first biographer, claimed in The Life of Thomas Jefferson that

the recollections of Meck Dec signers were, in fact, pilfered inter-
polations from Jefferson's own declaration, and that no backwoods
farmers could have anticipated the call for independence more
than a year before the Sage of Monticello. This brought counter-
charges from North Carolina clergyman Francis L. Hawks, who
claimed that Jefferson had stolen his words from the Meck Dec.
The argument was taken up in the pages of the Southern Literary Messenger, the Richmond magazine that was an outlet for the
young Edgar Allan Poe, from which the following account is taken.
The first part is a sidebar by the Messenger's editor, stating the
magazine's belief in the authenticity of the Meck Dec and printing
a copy of the declaration itself. The second is an essay contributed
by a mysterious "C. L. H." that traces the political history of North
Carolina leading up to the Meck Dec in an attempt to show how
Mecklenburg's farmers and traders would have been pushed to call
for independence.

Whatever the true story of the Meck Dec, May 20 is still
celebrated in Mecklenburg County and North Carolina as the day
when the Old North State became "First in Freedom." The date
May 20, 1775, appears on both the seal and the flag of the state
of North Carolina. Mecklenburg observes Meck Dec Day on
May 20 each year; the celebrations have waned from their peak
in the mid-20th century, when President Dwight D. Eisenhower
came to visit, but the recently formed May 20th Society has begun
aggressively promoting the day and the Meck Dec with speakers
and community events.

As this is the second notice taken in the *Messenger* of the Mecklenburg Declaration, and as it is, in itself, a very curious Revolutionary and Literary relic, we have thought it might gratify the curiosity of our readers to lay it before them. The following is a copy of it, taken from Mr. G. Tucker's *Life of Thomas Jefferson*, etc.

"The Mecklenburg Declaration of Independence (20th of May, 1775)

"That whosoever directly or indirectly abets, or in any way, form, or manner, countenances the unchartered and dangerous invasion of our rights, as claimed by Great Britain, is an enemy to this country, to America, and to the inherent and undeniable rights of man.

"That we, the citizens of Mecklenburg county, do hereby dissolve the political bands, which have connected us with the mother country, and hereby absolve ourselves from all allegiance to the British crown, and abjure all political connexion, contract, or association with that nation, who have wantonly trampled on our rights and liberties, and inhumanly shed the blood of American patriots at Lexington.

"That we do hereby declare ourselves a free and independent people; are, and of right ought to be, a sovereign and self-governing association, under the control of no power, other than that of our God, and the general government of Congress; to the maintenance of which independence, we solemnly pledge to each other, our mutual co-operation, our lives, our fortunes, and our most sacred honor.

"That as we acknowledge the existence and control of no law nor legal officer, civil or military, within this county, we do hereby ordain and adopt as a rule of life, all, each, and every of our former laws; wherein, nevertheless, the crown of Great Britain never can be considered as holding rights, privileges, immunities, or authority therein.

"That it is further decreed, that all, each, and every military officer in this county, is hereby reinstated in his former command and authority, while acting conformably to the regulations. And that every member present of this delegation shall henceforth be a civil officer, viz. a justice of the peace, in the character of a committee man, to issue process, hear, and determine all matters of controversy, according to said adopted laws; and to preserve peace, union, and harmony in said county, and to use every exertion to spread the love of country and fire of freedom throughout America, until a more general and organized government be established in this province.

Abraham Alexander, Chairman
John McKnitt Alexander, Secretary"

It is our misfortune to differ with Mr. Tucker about the character of this document. He is anxious to justify Mr. Jefferson against the charge of plagiarism, and he contends that the charge is the other way; that the Mecklenburg Declaration has been altered, both in its scope and expressions, from its original cast; that the two paragraphs in which the coincidence (between the Mecklenburg Declaration and Mr. J.'s Declaration) is found, have been subsequently interpolated, with a view of enhancing the merit of the act, and of making it a more unequivocal Declaration of Independence! . . .

We think, on the other hand, that all the propositions stand in their natural order; that the one grows necessarily out of the other, as conclusions following their premises. . . .

But, though we cannot subscribe to Mr. T.'s suppositions, still we agree with him in his main object. We clear Mr. Jefferson of the charge of plagiarism, as we have shown in our April No.

The April number of the *Southern Literary Messenger* contains a spirited article, entitled "The New York Review of Mr. Jefferson Reviewed." In the course of the reviewer's remarks, allusion is made to the Mecklenburg Declaration of Independence, adopted on the 20th of May, 1775. As the issue there presented is clothed in rather a mystical garb, and as the subject is still new, and imperfectly understood by many in our common country, we have been induced to believe that a condensed view of this novel and interesting transaction would be acceptable to the readers of the *Messenger*, and impart summary information to those who have not examined the testimony adduced in its favor. Wherever an impartial investigation has been instituted on this subject by the candid inquirer after truth, the universal conviction has been that the Mecklenburg Resolves are an original and bona fide Declaration of Independence; and, as such, claim priority over all others. However sensitive the acknowledged author of the National Declaration was, on the first announcement of this subject in 1819, and whatever skepticism others may now exhibit, yet the venerable maxim, "Truth is powerful and will prevail," conveys salutary advice, and requires only time, in this instance, to receive additional confirmation. We are fully disposed to render to Mr. Jefferson all that meed [reward] of approbation to which his eminent services justly entitle him; but, at the same time, wish to guard against that overweening attachment or parasitical admiration for a distinguished name which would make us partial in our decisions. . . .

. . . Without, therefore, pretending to award the palm of victory to either, we leave the matter where we find it, before the public tribunal . . . and shall acquiesce in their decision.

At an early period in the history of North Carolina may be traced manifest signs of that spirit of freedom and secret aspirations after liberty, which afterwards shone out in all their meridian splendor. The great distance of the mother country—the absence of royal magnificence—the free exercise of religious opinions—the general mediocrity of society—the numerous obstacles surmounted in settling a wilderness and securing a home, all tended to produce among the colonies a sense of self-dependence, and render them averse to every species of superiority or domination. They were so many excitants in awakening successful enterprise, and gradually unfolding to view a progressive development of national pride. From these causes and others of collateral tendency, originated an early conviction that all men were "created equal," endowed with certain "inalienable" or "inherent rights," and entitled to certain "exclusive privileges." When it was resolved by Parliament on the 10th of March, 1764, to raise a revenue in the colonies by a system of taxation, the delicate cord of "national rights" was sensibly touched, and ceased not to vibrate until the disturbing cause was removed. On the 31st of October following, we find the popular house of the assembly of North Carolina, in their address to the Governor, openly avowing its injustice and unconstitutionality. On the passage of the Stamp

Act in 1765, the citizens of North Carolina exhibited, in common with the other colonies, an unqualified disapprobation of the "odious measure," and a stern and unyielding opposition to its execution within her borders.... From the 3rd of April, 1765, to the 1st of July, 1771, North Carolina was governed by William Tryon. During the whole term of his administration, the public mind was agitated by the passage of the Stamp Act. Tryon met his first assembly one month after entering upon the duties of his office. Rumors and reports from the North currently prevailed among the people, that the Stamp Act had been passed by Parliament. This intelligence reached Wilmington shortly after the meeting of the assembly; and such was the violence exhibited by the members of the popular house, that Governor Tryon suddenly prorogued [discontinued] the legislative body on the 18th of the same month in which it had assembled....

... We will now advert [refer] to a few important transactions in the administration of Josiah Martin, Tryon's successor, and the last of the royal Governors. On the 19th of November, 1771, Martin met his first assembly. At each session of the assembly, from the year 1771 to 1774, inclusive, there occurred a quarrel with the Governor, invariably terminating in a prorogation of that body. These prorogations or dissolutions uniformly grew out of the adoption of some high-toned resolution, or the passage of some bill on the several local questions which agitated the province. After the dissolution of the assembly, in the spring of 1774, the situation of the province was little short of anarchy. The total disregard to the wants of the people on the part of the Governor could not fail to produce the most intense excitement. Owing to this incessant source of vexation, and the universal discontent that prevailed, we find the principal Whig leaders of that day busily engaged in maturing plans for the organization of a provincial Congress. . . . When the project of a provincial and continental Congress was published abroad, the people embraced it with enthusiasm and zeal. About the 1st of July handbills were circulated throughout the province, inviting the people to elect delegates to a convention. . . . The delegates punctually met in New Bern on the 25th of August, 1774. This was the first provincial Congress. The interesting proceedings on that occasion can receive in this sketch nothing more than a passing notice. The several acts of Parliament, imposing duties on imports, were condemned as highly illegal and oppressive; the inhabitants of Massachusetts province were applauded for distinguishing themselves in a "manly support of the rights of America in general"; and resolutions proposing to carry into execution any general plan of commercial restrictions agreed to in the continental Congress were adopted. It was further resolved that William Hooper, Joseph Hewes, and Richard Caswell, be appointed deputies to attend the General Congress, to be held in Philadelphia on the 20th of September following; and to be "invested with such powers, as may make any act done by them obligatory in honor upon every inhabitant of the province, who is not an alien to his country's good, and an apostate to the liberties of America." The second provincial Congress convened in New Bern on the 3rd of April, 1775. . . . This was the last assembly that ever convened under the royal government. . . .

After the dissolution of the assembly, the Governor found himself surrounded by only a few of his most faithful councilors. The royal government was now tottering to its base, and signs of a fatal decay were everywhere visible. In the meantime, the Governor, finding it inexpedient to issue writs of election for a new assembly, busily engaged himself in fortifying his palace, and raising a military force. . . . While the Governor and Council were in session in the palace, some of the leading Whigs seized and carried off the artillery which had been planted for its defense. "Governor Martin, apprehending further violence from the Whig leaders, on the evening of the same day, fled from the palace; and, accompanied by a few of his most faithful councilors, retreated to Fort Johnson on the banks of the Cape Fear." He did not, however, find the fort a much safer position for his headquarters than the palace at New Bern. In this retreat he was vigorously pursued, and forced to remove his military stores, as well as the headquarters of his government, on board "his Majesty's ship-of-war *Cruiser.*" The flight of his Excellency from the palace at New Bern, on the 24th of April, 1775, may be marked as the closing scene of the royal government. "During the spring of this year, 1775, the attention of all the colonies was directed towards Boston, a town which seemed to be the object of the devoted vengeance of the ministry." Several detached meetings of the people of Mecklenburg were held during the spring, in which it was declared, "that the cause of Boston was the cause of all"; and "that their destinies were indissolubly connected with those of their eastern fellow-citizens." Out of this state of feeling grew the Mecklenburg Declaration of Independence. The convention which assembled in Charlotte on the 19th of May, 1775, and declared independence on the succeeding 20th, was convoked [summoned] by Col. Thomas Polk, who afterwards performed the office of a herald, in proclaiming its proceedings "to a large, respectable, and approving assemblage of citizens." "The subject of independence was discussed during the two days of its session, and was at last unanimously declared. The news of the battle of Lexington arrived by express during the session of the convention; and this intelligence inflaming the minds of the people, the universal voice was for independence." The flame thus kindled at Lexington continued to spread through the province with unabated fury. . . . After Governor Martin was expelled from the province, and forced to take shelter on board his Majesty's ship-of-war *Cruiser*, and whilst this declaration, by the citizens of Mecklenburg, was still ringing unpleasantly in royal ears, he issued a lengthy proclamation—the last dying effort of fallen, but struggling authority. In this furious document, after reciting several "traitorous proceedings" of the people, he uses the following language: "And, whereas, I have also seen a most infamous publication in the Cape Fear *Mercury*, importing to be resolves of a set of people styling themselves a committee for the county of Mecklenburg, most traitorously declaring the entire dissolution of the laws, government and constitution of this country, and setting up a system of rule and regulation repugnant to the laws and subversive of his Majesty's government." This extract cannot be viewed by the most skeptical inquirer as otherwise than affording impartial and contemporaneous evidence. Another high source of authority attesting the identity of this declaration is to be found in the manuscript "Journal of the War in the South," by the late Rev. Humphrey Hunter, who was an eyewitness of the proceedings of that day, and a soldier of the Revolution. . . . We deem it unnecessary to analyze particularly the various sources of evidence, any one of which justly merits respectful consideration. The certificate of Captain James Jack, who bore the declaration to Congress, then in session at Philadelphia; a letter from the late General Joseph Graham, a soldier of the Revolution, and covered with scars in its defense; the personal testimony of the late Colonel William Polk of Raleigh; and a letter from John Davidson, the last surviving signer, have all been adduced to confirm its adoption, and constitute a mass of high and indisputable testimony. Numerous events in our Revolutionary history, which have received the stamp of universal belief for more than half a century, cannot present a more formidable phalanx of irresistible proof.

In the article above referred to, the serious inquiry has been raised, "How is it possible that this paper, if it reached Congress, was concealed?" To this we answer in the language of the "Journal," just mentioned, that "on the return of Captain Jack, he reported that Congress, individually, manifested their entire approbation of the conduct of the Mecklenburg citizens, but deemed it premature to lay them officially before the house." In other words, the citizens of Mecklenburg, and of the state generally, were more than one year in advance of the other colonies in a determination to declare independence. At that period Congress had not arrived at sufficient maturity of opinion as to ensure unanimity of action on a question so momentous, and on the determination of which depended the destiny of the nation. There were many distinguished patriots who still ardently entertained hopes of an amicable adjustment of difficulties with the mother country; but in North Carolina pacific measures were out of the question. . . . The question has been likewise asked, why it should remain unknown so long afterwards? To this we answer that few copies of such a paper would be prepared at first, and consequently, still fewer would escape the ravages of time. These, through the careless researches of historians, have remained concealed until within a few years past. . . .

We have now presented a brief outline of the train of proceedings leading to the adoption of the Mecklenburg Declaration of Independence on the 20th of May, 1775. If we have succeeded in imparting information, invalidating objections, or removing prejudice from the mind of any one on this subject, our humble, though laudable, ambition, will be fully satisfied, and our limited exertions amply rewarded.

C. L. H.

NOTES

[1]*Southern Literary Messenger* 4, no. 7 (Richmond, Va.: T. W. White, Editor and Proprietor, 1838): 481–86.

Persuading the Back Country

By William Henry Drayton and
the Reverend William Tennent[1]

For most of South Carolina's colonial history, the rice kings
of the Low Country paid little mind to their fellow Carolinians
in the interior. Historian Walter Edgar puts it this way: "At best,
backcountry folk were treated as second-class citizens; at worst,
they were simply the first line of defense against the Indians."[2] As
the relationship with Great Britain deteriorated, though, the Whig
planters realized they would need the support of the back country, where most white South Carolinians lived. In the summer of
1775, the Provincial Congress sent a delegation to the back country to persuade its inhabitants to join the cause of liberty. Five men
were chosen: Oliver Hart, a Baptist minister; Joseph Kershaw and

Richard Richardson, two of the back country's leading Whigs; the Reverend William Tennent, a Presbyterian minister; and one of the greatest of the rice kings, William Henry Drayton.

They faced a formidable task. The back country was already divided into communities of geography, ethnicity, and economic interest, and those communities were further divided by the question of independence. Some remained loyal to the Crown out of natural conservatism or fear of losing a royal land grant; some remained loyal because they saw the colonies' quarrels with England as a Low Country problem that did not concern them. While many back-country leaders, such as Kershaw, Richardson, William Hill (see "Huck's Defeat," pages 89-94), and William Thomson, threw their support behind the Provincial Congress, plenty more—notably Thomas Fletchall, Moses Kirkland, and Robert Cunningham—announced their intention never to oppose their rightful king. The vast majority in the back country, though, "if they had had their druthers . . . would just like to have been left alone."[3]

Drayton had lived his life at the very pinnacle of South Carolina society. Like many young rice kings, he was educated in England (at Westminster School and Balliol College, Oxford). In fact, in the 1760s and early 1770s, he was such a vociferous defender of the Crown that he left South Carolina to return to England. This sojourn, however, may have turned the king's friend into the ardent Whig he became. "In England," historian John Buchanan notes, "he was just another colonial, and it has been suggested that he returned home in 1772 with the bitter taste reserved by the British aristocracy for colonials whatever their status at home."[4] Drayton would serve South Carolina as a judge, chief justice, congressman, and architect of the battery on Sullivan's Island (see "Account of the Attack on Fort Moultrie," pages 37-50).

Drayton and his party spent August and September touring the back country in a series of meetings, some of which took on the character and feel of religious revivals, with the clergymen Hart and Tennent preaching long sermons on liberty and tyranny. Near the start of their journey, Drayton and Tennent sent the following report back to Charleston.

From Drayton and Tennent
Congaree Store, August 7th, 1775
To the Council of Safety

Gentlemen:

Having left Charles Town on Wednesday morning, we arrived here early on Saturday afternoon, 130 miles distant from town. In our way, we spent some hours at Col. Gaillard's, and we flatter ourselves the visit had a good effect. It is to be hoped, he has not delivered himself in public so warmly, as he has expressed himself to us.

Upon our arrival at the Congaree Store, we found two gentlemen of the bar, John Dunn, and Benj. Booth or Boote, prisoners from North Carolina, who had arrived here the evening before, from the committee at Camden. For other particulars on this subject, we beg leave to refer you to our letter of this date addressed to the General Committee. As a first step to the particular object of our progress, upon our arrival here, we dispatched notices to particular persons of influence among the Dutch [Germans], to endeavor to procure a meeting of them at the place of election as on this day. To our great mortification not one German appeared, but one or two of our friends who had been industrious to procure a meeting. By them we were informed, their countrymen were so much averse to take up arms, as they imagined, against the king, least they should lose their lands; and were so possessed with an idea that the rangers were posted here to force their signatures to the association, that they would not by any arguments be induced to come near us. Add to this, that a report had ran among them, that we had brought up orders to let the rangers loose upon them to destroy their properties. However unfavorable these circumstances are, we hope you will not be alarmed at them; we yet have some hopes of success, though we confess they are but small in this quarter.

We have engaged Col. Thomson to order a muster of two Dutch companies in this neighborhood on Wednesday next, and we have declared if the officers disobey they shall be broke. This threat was highly necessary, as the Dutch Captains had some little time ago disobeyed such an order, alleging that extra musters were warranted only by orders from the Governor. We hope this step will oblige a part of the Germans to give us a hearing; and as we flatter ourselves that our discourses to them will not be entirely lost upon them, we expect these will induce others of their countrymen to be willing to hear what we have to say. With this view, and to give such persons an opportunity of hearing us, we have engaged one Dutch clergyman to perform service at one place on Friday next, and another, at a second place on Sunday next, at both which places Mr. Drayton will be present. And in the mean time, as we know in general, that an argument relating to money matters most readily catches a Dutchman's ear, we have declared that no non-subscriber in this settlement will be allowed to purchase at, or sell to this store or Charles Town. When Mr. Drayton shall quit the Dutch settlements on Sunday next, after having had on Saturday a meeting with a large number of people of all sorts, at one McLaurin's, a store keeper, hitherto an enemy, but now, at least in appearance, a friend, he will proceed up the fork to Col. Fletchall's, at which place he may arrive on Tuesday. While Mr. Drayton shall be thus proceeding in the fork between Broad and Saluda rivers, Mr. Tennent will, on Wednesday set out to proceed through the [Scots-]Irish settlements on the north side of Broad river up to Rocky Creek and thence join Mr. Drayton at or near Col. Fletchall's. Those settlements are numerous and ready to sign the Association.

We have various accounts respecting the disposition of the people in Fletchall's quarters; some say we will not be heard. Indeed, we expect much trouble; however, we flatter ourselves that we shall one way or other meet with success. We have dispatched proper persons before us, who we doubt not will much contribute to prepare the minds of the people to hear us favorably. Mr. Hart has just come up to us with another clergyman of his persuasion. These gentlemen will to-morrow proceed towards Fletchall's quarters. We have consulted with Col. Richardson touching Mr. [Thomas] Sumter's application to the Council. The Colonel readily approved not only of the measure, but of the man, notwithstanding Kirkland recommended him as his successor in the company of Rangers, which he has so treacherously quitted and attempted to disband. The Colonel, nevertheless, from his seeming connection with Kirkland, purposes to keep a sharp eye upon Mr. Sumter's conduct.[5]

Yesterday Mr. Tennent performed divine service in camp; and in the afternoon Mr. Drayton harangued the Rangers respecting the new and extraordinary power by which they were raised; the nature of the public disputes, and the justice of the cause in which they were engaged, the nature of their allegiance to the King and their duty to their country, their families and themselves; their duty and obligation to oppose and attack any British troops landing in this colony; their honor was awakened by contrasting their personal value and importance against the importance of the British troops; their complaints respecting provisions were entered into, and they were assured the public meant to do all that could be done for them consistently with the nature of discipline and the calamitous situation of affairs; they were informed that the public could not so much dishonor them as to imagine they had enlisted merely for pecuniary gain, but persuaded that they being actuated with a nobler motive, all men were willing to believe, that they without wishing to be at ease in every respect, as in a regular service under an established and quiet Government, did not, as they could not in honor or conscience, desire more than absolute necessaries. And that, if they thought it a hardship to go abroad to procure provisions, the Council were ready to save them that trouble by deducting a reasonable sum from their pay, and supplying them with provisions in the manner in which the foot [soldiers] were furnished. They had grumbled about tents, and were now informed that the British troops in America during the last war, not only generally used but preferred huts made of bushes.

Finally, encomiums were passed upon the progress they had made in the art military, and it was recommended to them in the strongest terms to pay the most perfect obedience to their officers, as the only means by which they could become good soldiers, and to defend those liberties and rights which they appeared so willing to protect. Hitherto there has been but little subordination.

To these things Mr. Tennent added assurances of the value of Congress currency which many people had endeavored to depreciate in the opinion of the soldiers, and he read and commented upon the declaration of the General Congress.

These things being finished, we left the camp in apparent quiet satisfaction and content, the men on being discharged expressing their thanks to us. But about midnight, an officer stole from the camp (about two miles off) and gave us the most alarming intelligence that a most dangerous mutiny had broke out in, and prevailed throughout the whole camp, in which there was no longer any command or obedience; that the men were in an uproar at the idea of a deduction of their pay, for they had in general been promised provisions above their pay, and they were determined to quit the camp this morning and disband. Col. Thomson and Capt. Kershaw lodge[d] with us; they were willing to do any thing that was thought proper. We consulted with them upon the case, and it was thought most advisable not to take any step in the night or for either of those officers to go to the camp; but that time should be allowed for the men to cool, and for the three Captains and other officers in camp to sound the men, and learn who would be depended upon. This measure had the effect we expected, and this morning the men appeared quiet, and it became evident that the disorders arose from three or four privates of profligate dispositions, and from improper conduct, declarations, and conversations of some officers. Capt. Woodward had incautiously [enlisted] his men, made promises which proved grounds of discontent and disappointment, and yesterday had even the rashness to attempt to be spokesman to us in the hearing of the Rangers in favor of their being found above their pay; and Lieutenant Dutarque, also attempted to inveigh against the cruelty of keeping men encamped without tents. Such topics had by these officers frequently been touched upon heretofore, but we have privately given them a lecture upon the subject, and we hope as they heard us in a proper manner, that it will have a good effect. From such sources, however, it is plain the disorder of last night arose. The Rangers were this morning marched from camp to this place, where Mr. Drayton harangued them upon the disorder of the last night, attributing it to a few disorderly persons, who in this the first instance, would by the Colonel be passed over unnoticed, in hopes such lenity would work a reformation in them. The consequences of a mutinous conduct were described as tending to expose them to the derision of their neighbors and enemies, and to cover them and the whole corps with shame, contempt, infamy and ruin, without effecting the public service; for, if they should prove unworthy of the service, they would certainly be brought to condign [fitting] punishment, and other and more worthy rangers be found to supply their places. For they ought not to flatter themselves that because some parts of this country were disaffected, that therefore they could desert and be in places of security. If any should desert they must some time be off their caution and guard, and then they would be seized, for a reward would be put upon their heads; no money would be thought too much to ferret them out wheresoever they should go; and dead or alive they would certainly be carried to Charles Town. The situation of America was placed before them. On one side of the question stood almost infinite numbers, supported by wealth and men of learning and abilities to plan and execute measures to overcome their opponents, who, of the Americans were only a few men of little property and less knowledge and abilities to conduct affairs; and they were asked, if they could possibly think there was any safety among such men. The obligation of their oath was strongly insisted upon; and as to provisions, it was declared that the officers would endeavor to encourage people, of whom many were willing to supply the camp; in which case the soldiers should purchase as they pleased in camp, where, when there were any provisions they should not be allowed to go abroad to seek what they could find at home. They were told, they were not now to look for rewards, but that they must expect them when these troubles were over. For, as in the mean time it would be known who among them behaved with due obedience, and who conducted themselves otherwise; so, all these things in time to come would be remembered by the gentlemen below, who would in private affairs show to the first all kinds of favors and acts of friendship whenever opportunities should offer; and they would carefully mark the latter, and discountenance and thwart them upon every occasion. This discourse we flatter ourselves had a full effect. They were called upon to say what they pleased; except three men, they were all well satisfied and contented, and showed the most perfect submission. These three were properly checked, and the worst of them severely reprimanded and spoken to in private.

We have thus given a particular account of our conduct to

the troops and the nature of our discourse to them; by which, you will be enabled to have an idea of the method in which we purpose to discharge the duties of our journey. If we have done any thing amiss, or have been deficient in treating the subject, be pleased to make your observations and we shall endeavor to conduct ourselves accordingly.

As well to remove the apprehensions of the Dutch settlers as those of the interior parts, that the Rangers were posted here to force measures; and to remove every idea that we came up to issue orders to plunder and lay waste, as well as to allow the soldiers to go home to places of election, and to procure necessaries, and to show that we place a confidence in their good behavior, we have this day broken up the camp and sent them to their respective homes under their officers, with orders to repair to a new camp in Amelia about thirty miles below this, and to join there on the 18th inst., at which place Maj. Mason is likewise under orders to appear at the same time with Capt. Purvis's Company. For the Major's personal presence in Ninety-Six is of disservice to the public affairs.

We find that Moses Kirkland is gone to town to the Governor; we have issued private directions to apprehend him in his return home, in hopes of taking upon him some papers from the Governor, as it is generally suspected he has gone to procure proper authorities from Lord William [Campbell] to counteract and oppose the provincial proceedings. Whether he has these papers or not, he will, if taken, be carried to you; for, if upon searching him, no papers shall be found, it may be of evil consequence to set him at liberty to continue his journey home; for, as he is very active in poisoning the minds of the people, he will greatly interrupt our proceedings to compose them. At any rate, he ought to appear before you to answer for his conduct in disbanding his men; and such a step will have good effect, as it will show vigor in government, and will have no tendency to alarm the non-subscribers up here, because Kirkland, from his own act and consent is amenable to the law military.

With regard to Capt. Polk, we are at present silent, but we hope you will not delay to fill up Captain's Commissions for those two vacancies, by promoting the two eldest first lieutenants, as in such a case Mr. Heatly will speedily procure full compliments of recruits for himself. We also beg leave to inform you that a Surgeon's mate is necessary for the Rangers, although there is no provision for such a post by particular act of Congress, yet it may arise from your power, as such an officer is, in our opinion and the Colonel's, necessary for the service. We beg leave to recommend Lieutenant Thomas Charlton, a man of experience and reputation in physic [medicine], and who came into the corps under an idea, that there was provision for such an appointment. He is worthy of the first post in that line in the regiment; but being willing to serve the public in this cause, he is content with the last rank in the way of his profession.

We are like to incur a heavy expense in horses. For Mr. Hart and ourselves five were purchased in Charles Town. One of these we have been obliged to swap. . . . Three others have failed so much that we are obliged to purchase others, and leave these with Col. Thomson to dispose of, at the best rate. We shall draw upon you for these three to be purchased, as we do not cho[o]se to make so large a disbursement out of the sum in our hands, as also for two others, to accommodate Mr. Hart's companion and Mr. Tennant's excursion. These horses are good, and in all probability will sell after we have done with them, for more money than they have cost the public.

> We are, gentlemen,
> Your most humble servts.,
>
> Wm. H. Drayton,
> Wm. Tennent

P.S. The Rangers perform their exercise at least as well as the Regulars in Charles Town; and we have taken the liberty to open a public letter to Col. [John] Laurens from Col. Fletchall.

Notes

[1] R. W. Gibbes, *Documentary History of the American Revolution*, vol. 1 (New York: D. Appleton & Co., 1855), 128–33.

[2] Walter Edgar, *Partisans and Redcoats: The Southern Conflict That Turned the Tide of the American Revolution* (New York: Harper Perennial, 2003), 29.

[3] Ibid., 30.

[4] John Buchanan, *The Road to Guilford Courthouse: The American Revolution in the Carolinas* (New York: John Wiley & Sons, 1997), 23.

[5] Nathanael Greene and others might have wished someone had kept a closer eye on Thomas Sumter, but not because of possible disloyalty; see "The Gamecock," pages 95-100.

The Making of a Tory Partisan

From *The Narrative of Colonel David Fanning*[1]

While the Reverend William Tennent preached and exhorted
in the back country, William Henry Drayton alternated attempts
at persuasion with threats of force. These eventually resulted in the
Treaty of Ninety-Six, in which the Provincial Congress agreed to
leave back-country loyalists alone, as long as they remained neutral
in the event of armed conflict.

Drayton broke the treaty before he even left the back country,
taunting Robert Cunningham and other Tory leaders in a calculated attempt to provoke a response.[2] When Drayton's calculations
proved correct, he had Cunningham and the others arrested and
taken to Charleston. The royal governor, Lord William Campbell,

had already left Charleston to seek shelter on a British warship anchored in Charleston Harbor. The Provincial Congress, led by Governor John Rutledge, ruled South Carolina.

In October, back-country Tories revolted against the Provincial Congress, capturing a Whig convoy carrying powder and lead. Major Andrew Williamson led 500 South Carolina militia in an attempt to recapture the supplies; finding himself outnumbered, though, he built a defensive position at the back-country outpost of Ninety-Six. The Tories attacked and took the fort at Ninety-Six in November. The Revolutionary War in South Carolina had begun.

The Provincial Congress responded by sending Richard Richardson (a member of Drayton's back-country delegation) and 3,000 militia against the Tories. In late December, in the midst of a 30-inch snowfall, Richardson surprised and routed the Tories at the Battle of the Great Cane Break in what is now Greenville. The Snow Campaign was over, but the partisan war in the back country was just beginning.

David Fanning was one of the most active combatants in the partisan war. Having sworn his loyalty to King George III even before Drayton and Tennent came to the back country, he continued to prove that loyalty even after Lord Cornwallis surrendered at Yorktown. Born in 1755 in Virginia and orphaned in 1764, he grew up in North Carolina in the care of a county justice. In 1773, he moved to the back country of South Carolina. After the war, he moved to Florida and then the Bahamas before settling in Canada. He died in Nova Scotia in 1825.[3]

The following excerpt from his memoir of his service in the war begins with an address to the reader justifying his loyalty to the Crown. Fanning goes on to tell of how he became a loyalist *partisan, of his participation in the siege of Ninety-Six and the Battle of the Great Cane Break, of his flight to the Cherokees, and of the first three of his many captures.*

To the Reader:

Courteous Reader, whoever thou art, the Author being only a Farmer bred, and not conversant in learning, thou mayst think that the within Journal is not authentic. But it may be depended upon that every particular herein mentioned is nothing but the truth; Yea, I can boldly assert that I have undergone much more than what is herein mentioned.

Rebellion according to Scripture is as the sin of witchcraft; and the propagators thereof, has more than once punished; which is dreadfully exemplified this day in the now United States of America but formerly Provinces; for since their Independence from Great Britain, they have been awfully and visibly punished by the fruits of the earth being cut off; and civil dissension every day prevailing among them; their fair trade, and commerce almost totally ruined; and nothing prospering so much as nefarious and rebellious smuggling. Whatever imperfections is in the within, [it is] hoped will be kindly overlooked by the courteous Reader, and attributed to the Author's want of learning.

I do not set forth any thing as a matter of amusement, but what is really, justly fact, that my transactions and scenes of life have been as herein narrated during the term of the Rebellion; and that conduct, resolution, and courage perform wondrous things beyond credibility, the following of which laudable deeds will give them, are exercised there in the experience that I have gained.

In the 19th year of my age, I entered into the war; and proceeded from one step to another, as is herein mentioned, and at the conclusion thereof, was forced to leave the place of my nativity for my adherence to the British Constitution; and after my sore fatigues, I arrived at St. John River; and there with the blessing of God, I have hitherto enjoyed the sweets of peace, and freedom under the benevolent auspices of the British Government which every loyal and true subject may enjoy with me, is the wish of the Author.

David Fanning
King's County
Long Beach
New Brunswick
June 24th 1790

Colonel Thomas Fletchall of Fairforest ordered the different Captains to call musters, and present two papers for the inhabitants to sign. One was to see who was friends to the King and Government; and the other was to see who would join the Rebellion.

The first day of May, Capt. James Lindley of Rabern's Creek, sent to me, as I was a Sergeant of the said company, to have his company warned to meet at his house 15th of said month. I did accordingly, and presented two papers; there was 118 men signed in favor of the King, also declared to defend the same, at the risk of lives and property, in July 1775. There was several advertisements set up in every part of said district, that there was a very good prespetearing [Presbyterian] minister [probably William Tennent; see "Persuading the Back Country," pages 16-27] to call at the different places, to preach, and baptize children.

But at the time appointed, instead of meeting a minister, we all went to meet two Jews by name of Silvedoor and Rapely; and after making many speeches in favor of the Rebellion, and us[ing] all their endeavors to delude the people away, at last presented Revolution papers to see who would sign them; they were severely reprimanded by Henry O'Neal and many others. It came so high, that they had much ado to get off with their lives. The Rebels then found that we were fully determined to oppose them. They began to embody in the last of said month; to compel all to join them, or to take away our arms. Our officers got word of their intentions. I then got orders from the Captain to warn the Militia to assemble themselves at Hugh O'Neal's mill; which was done by several Captain's companies, and continued for several days under arms; and then both parties was determined on this condition, that neither parties should intercept each other. This continued for some time, until the Rebels had taken Thomas Brown, who after that had the honor to be Colonel of the Regiment of the East Florida Rangers, at Augusta. They burnt his feet, tarred, feathered and cut off his hair. After that he got so he was able to set on horseback, he came to our post, and the Rebels then began to embody again. Col. Fletchall found a large camp, and marched from the Liberty Springs to Mill Creek on our way towards Ninety-Six. Twelve miles from Ninety-Six, the Rebels found they were not strong enough for us, and sent an express to Col. Fletchall to come and treat with them, which said Fletchall did. But the terms of their treatment I did not know. We were all dismissed until farther orders. In a short time after[,] the Rebels took Capt. Robert Cunningham and carried him off to Charleston. Our party was then informed of his being taken off in the night time, and by making inquiry after him, we got information of a large quantity of ammunition, that was there, on its way to the Cherokee Nation for Capt. Richard Paris[4] to bring the Indians down into the settlement, where the friends of the Government lived, to murder all they could. We intercepted the ammunition and took Capt. R. Paris, who swore to these facts. We there formed a large camp, and Col. Fletchall being so heavy, he gave up the command to Maj. Joseph Robinson.

In the month of November, 1775, the South Carolina Militia, of which I was at that time Sergeant, under the command of Major Joseph Robinson, laid siege to a fort, erected by the Rebels at Ninety-Six; commanded by Col. Mason: which continued for the space of three days, and three nights at the expiration of which time the Rebels were forced to surrender, and give up the Fort and Artillery. Major Robinson then ordered the Militia to the north side of Saluda River, and discharged them, for eighteen days. Afterwards orders were issued for every Captain to collect their respective companies at Hendrick's Mill, about 20 miles from Ninety-Six; the Rebels having received intelligence of our intended motion, they immediately marched before us, and took possession of the ground, which prevented our assembling there. But about 300 of our men met at Little River and marched from thence to Reedy River, and encamped at the Big Cane Break, for several days. The

Rebels, being informed of our situation, marched unexpectedly upon us, and made prisoners of 130 of [our] men; the remainder fled into the woods and continued there, with the Cherokee Indians until the 18th January, 1776; when I was made a prisoner by a party of Rebels commanded by a Captain John Burns, who, after detaining me four days, repeatedly urging me to take the oath of allegiance to the United States, stripped me of every thing, and made me give security, for my future good behavior, by which means I got clear. On the 10th of May, 1776, hearing the Rebels had issued a proclamation to all the friends of government, offering them pardon and protection, provided they would return to their respective habitations and remain neutral, this induced me for to return to my home, where I arrived on the 15th of June.

On the 20th, the Rebels[,] being apprehensive of the Cherokee Indians breaking out, dispatched several emissaries among the Loyalists, for to discover their intentions. One of which was Capt. Ritchie, who came to me, and told me he was a friend to Government, and sometime before left the Indian Nation, and then wanted a pilot to conduct him to the Indian Nation again. I agreed to conduct him to any part of the country he wanted for to go to, provided he would keep it secret. This he promised for to do. But immediately he went and lodged information against me, and swore that I then had a company of men, ready in order, for to join the Indians. In consequence of this, I was made prisoner again, on the 25th, by a Capt. John Rogers, and thrown into close confinement with three sentinels over me. On the 1st of July, the Indians came down into the back country of South Carolina, and killed several families; at which time, the Rebel camp being in great confusion, I made my escape, and went to my own house at Rabern's creek; but finding a number of my friends had already gone to the Indians, and more disposed so for to do, I got twenty-five men to join me; and on our arrival at Paris's plantation, on Reedy River, in the Indian land, we formed a junction with the Indians, on the 16th inst., in the evening; the militia and the Cherokees to [the] amount of 260 surrounded the fort built with logs, containing 450 of the Rebels. After a smart fire on both sides for two hours and a half, we retreated without any injury except one of the Indian Chiefs being shot through the hand. I then left the Indians and pursued my way to North Carolina; where, on my arrival, I was taken up again, and close confined; but was rescued by my friends, three different times. After which I made my escape good. I then endeavored for to go home again; and after experiencing numberless hardships in the woods, I arrived the 10th of March, 1777, at Rabern's creek, South Carolina.

Notes

[1] David Fanning, *The Narrative of Colonel David Fanning, A Tory in the Revolutionary War with Great Britain* (New York: reprinted for Joseph Sabin, 1865), xxiii–4.

[2] Walter Edgar, *Partisans and Redcoats: The Southern Conflict That Turned the Tide of the American Revolution* (New York: Harper Perennial, 2003), 32.

[3] Robert S. Allen, *Dictionary of Canadian Biography Online* (University of Toronto, 2000), http://www.biographi.ca.

[4] Richard Pearis (often spelled Paris) was the first white settler in what is now Greenville County, South Carolina; Paris Mountain

is named after him. Though initially a Whig, he later switched to the Tories and was imprisoned in Charleston in 1776.

Account of the Attack on Fort Moultrie

From the *South Carolina and American General Gazette* of August 2, 1776[1]

By the summer of 1776, Whigs had taken control from the royal governors of all 13 colonies. Though Britain's focus remained on New England and the mid-Atlantic, ministers and officers in London decided that a quick strike to the south would rally loyalists and split the rebellious colonies. The government gave command of the southern district to General Sir Henry Clinton, who sailed from Boston to rendezvous at the mouth of the Cape Fear River with his second-in-command, Lieutenant General Charles, Earl Cornwallis, and seven regiments of British regulars. (Among these troops was unknown 22-year-old cavalry officer Banastre Tarleton.) Clinton's target was the wealthy harbor of Charleston, not the poor backwater of North Carolina, but Royal Governor Josiah Martin—now an exile from the colonial capital and governor in title only—convinced Clinton's superiors that North Carolina could easily be taken along the way. The plan put forward by Martin called for Clinton's regulars to link up with loyal Highland Scots from the interior settlement of Cross Creek, near what is now

Fayetteville. Sixteen hundred Scots led by Donald MacDonald set out for Wilmington in late February 1776.

In the swamps of southeastern North Carolina, about 1,000 rebels met the Scots at the bridge over Moores Creek. The rebels had removed half the planks from the bridge, greased the stringers with soap and tallow, and set up their position on the far side of the creek. MacDonald's deputy, Donald MacLeod, who had taken over battle command of the Highlanders, ordered 80 men armed only with broadswords to charge across the slippery half-bridge. The rebels waited until the Highlanders reached their side of the creek, then opened fire with cannon and muskets. Almost all the Highlanders were killed or captured.[2]

After some debate, Clinton and his force sailed on for Charleston, arriving off the bar before Charleston Harbor in June. They found the harbor's main defense, a fort on Sullivan's Island, only half finished; in fact, Charles Lee, the British-born general sent by the Continental Congress to defend Charleston, called the fort a "slaughter pen" and ordered it evacuated.[3] South Carolina governor John Rutledge and General William Moultrie, the commander of the fort and its garrison, ignored Lee's orders. On June 28, Lee attempted to reach Sullivan's Island by a small boat and to force Moultrie to abandon the fort, but rough water kept him from crossing until after the British began their assault.

The palmetto tree at the center of the South Carolina state flag commemorates the rebels' improbable victory at the Battle of Fort Sullivan. The half-finished slaughter pen was built of spongy palmetto logs, which absorbed the impact of the British cannonballs, rather than splintering as pine or oak logs would. Fort Sullivan was saved by more than palmetto logs, though. Clinton personally led a flanking force across the inlet between Long Island and Sullivan's Island, an inlet he had been told was easily fordable. It was not, and 780 rebels fended off Clinton's 2,200 redcoats. Meanwhile, three British warships ran aground on the shoal where Fort Sumter would later be built. Safe behind the palmetto logs, Moultrie's guns pounded away at the British ships. By midnight, the British fleet withdrew.

Moultrie was a Charleston native, a member of the Low Country aristocracy (his mother was a Cooper), and a veteran of the Cherokee War. He would survive the Revolutionary War to serve two terms as South Carolina's governor. After his brave defense of Sullivan's Island, the fort would be renamed Fort Moultrie in his honor.

The following account appeared in the South Carolina and American General Gazette, a leading newspaper, a little more than a month following the battle, after life had returned to some semblance of normalcy in Charleston. This lull would last nearly three and a half years, until the British once again set their sights on the Carolinas.

Charles Town, August 2, 1776

It having been deemed expedient that the printing presses should be removed out of town during the alarm, the publication of this *Gazette* has been necessarily discontinued for the last two months. As the transactions in this province during that period will probably make it a distinguished one in the American annals, we doubt not but a succinct account of them will be very acceptable to our readers.

On the 1st June, his Excellency, the President [John Rutledge], received advices of a fleet of forty or fifty sail being at anchor about six leagues to the northward of Sullivan's Island. Accounts of the arrival of Sir Peter Parker's fleet in North Carolina, and that it was destined either for Virginia or this province, having been received about three weeks before, put it beyond a doubt that this was his fleet. Next morning the alarm was fired, expresses having been sent ordering the country militia to town; the fortifications were all visited by his Excellency and Gen. [John] Armstrong, and preparations for the most vigorous defense ordered. In the evening a man-of-war, thought to [be] a twenty-gun ship, beat up to windward and anchored off the bar; next day she was joined by a frigate, and, on the day following, June 4, by upwards of fifty sail of men-of-war, transports, tenders, etc. We have since learned that the men-of-war were the *Bristol*, of 50 guns, on board of which the Commodore had his flag; the *Solebay*, Capt. Syrnonds, 28; *Syren*, Capt. Furneaux, 28; *Active*, Capt. Williams, 28; *Acteon*, Capt. Atkins, 28; *Sphinx*, Capt. Hunt, 20; *Hanger*, sloop, of 8; *Thunder Bomb*, of 6 guns and 2 mortars, one of them thirteen inches, and the other eleven; an armed ship, called the *Friendship*, of 18 Guns, with some smaller armed vessels. The same day Capt. Mowat arrived from North Carolina, with an express from General [Charles] Lee, informing that the fleet had left North Carolina, and that he would be here, as speedily as possible, with several Continental Regiments to our assistance.

A few days after the arrival of the fleet, several transports and small armed vessels went to Long Island, situated to the eastward of Sullivan's Island, from which it is separated by a small creek called the Breach, where they landed a large body of troops, who encamped there. The wind and tides being favorable for the four following days, about thirty-six vessels came over the bar, and anchored at about three miles' distance from Sullivan's Island. Two of their transports got aground in coming over; one got off, but the other went to pieces. On the 10th the *Bristol* came over, her guns being previously taken out.

On the 7th, a boat, with a flag of truce from the enemy, came towards the Island, but was fired on by an ignorant sentinel. The boat thereupon immediately put about, and would not return, notwithstanding the officer who was sent to receive the flag waved his handkerchief, and desired them to come ashore. Next day Col. Moultrie sent an officer to the fleet to acquaint them of the sentinel's having fired without orders, and that he was ready to receive anything they had to send.

Gen. Clinton was satisfied with the apology, and said the intention of the flag's being sent was only to deliver the following Proclamation, which the officer brought on shore:

A Proclamation by Major General Clinton, Commander of His Majesty's Forces in the Southern Provinces of North America, &c., &c.

Whereas, a most unprovoked and wicked rebellion hath for some time past prevailed, and doth now exist, within his Majesty's Province of South Carolina; and the inhabitants thereof, forgetting their allegiance to their sovereign, and denying the authority of the laws and statutes of the realm, have, in a succession of crimes, proceeded to the total subversion of all legal authority, usurping the powers of Government, and erecting a tyranny in the hands of Congresses and Committees of various denominations, utterly unknown and repugnant to the spirit of the British Constitution; and divers people, in avowed defiance to all legal authority, are now actually in arms, waging an unnatural war against the King. And whereas, all the attempts to reclaim the infatuated and misguided multitude to a sense of their error have hitherto unhappily proved ineffectual, I have it in command to proceed forthwith against all such men, or bodies of men in arms, and against all such Congresses and Committees thus unlawfully established, as against open enemies to the State. But, considering it as a duty inseparable from the principles of humanity, first of all to forewarn the deluded people of the miseries ever attendant upon civil war, I do most earnestly entreat and exhort them, as they tender their own happiness and that of their posterity, to return to their duty to our common sovereign, and to the blessings of a free Government, as established by law, hereby offering, in his Majesty's name, free pardon to all such as shall lay down their arms and submit to the laws: And I do hereby require that the Provincial Congress, and all Committees of Safety, and other unlawful associations, be dissolved, and the Judges allowed to hold their Courts according to the laws and Constitution of this Province, of which all persons are required to take notice, as they will answer the contrary at their peril.

Given on board the Sovereign transport, off Charles Town, this sixth day of June, 1776, and in the sixteenth year of his Majesty's reign.

> H. Clinton, Major-General
> By command of Gen. Clinton,
> Richard Reeve, Sec.

Major-General Lee, Brigadier-General [Robert] Howe, Colonel Bullet, Col. Jenifer, Otway Byrd and Lewis Morris, Esquires, aides-de-camp to General Lee, with some other gentlemen, arrived at Haddrel's Point on the morning of the 9th. After having viewed the fortifications there, and on Sullivan's and James Islands, they came to town. Orders being given on the 10th for a number of buildings on the wharfs to be pulled down, entrenchments to be thrown up all around the town, and barricades to be made in the principal streets every person, without distinction, were employed on these works.

On the 12th, there blew a violent storm, in which an hospital ship and the *Friendship*, which were at anchor on the other side of the bar, were obliged to put out to sea, but returned in a few days after. A schooner, having on board some provisions and coals, drifted a little way from the fleet, was taken by one of our pilot-boats, and brought to town. Her crew took to their boat on observing the pilot-boat approach.

His Excellency, the President, on the 14th, proposed to the militia under arms an oath of fidelity, which was voluntarily and readily taken by every one excepting three. The next morning it was proposed to the country militia doing duty in town, and to the Artillery Companies, when it met with their unanimous assent.

A sloop from the West Indies for this port, with a cargo of gunpowder, arms, rum, &c., having, on the afternoon of the 16th, descried the fleet, attempted to make her escape; but, through the ignorance of her pilot, ran aground and bilged. Next day she was discovered by the men-of-war, and a tender, with several boats full of armed men, came towards her. The crew, being only twenty-two men, unable to cope with such a force in the situation the vessel was in, quitted her. She was soon after boarded, set on fire, and blew up with a great explosion.

By some sailors who deserted from the Ranger sloop, lying near Long Island, we were informed that the land forces were about 2,800 (some say 3,300) men, under the command of Major-General Clinton, who had under him Major-General Lord Cornwallis and Brigadier-General [John] Vaughan.

On the 21st, our advanced party at the north-east end of Sullivan's Island fired several shot at the armed schooner, *Lady William*, an armed sloop, and a pilot-boat, lying in the creek between Long Island and the Main, several of which hulled them. For several mornings and evenings the enemy threw shells, and fired from some field pieces on our advanced post, but without any effect.

A large ship hove in sight on the 25th, in the morning. It was thought to be the *Roebuck*, but we have since learnt it was the *Experiment*, Capt. Scott, of 50 guns. Next day she came over, having her guns out. On the day following, the 27th, between nine and ten in the forenoon, as soon as the *Experiment* had her guns all in, the Commodore hoisted his topsails, fired a gun, and got under way. His example was followed by several others of the men-of-war; but a squall coming on, and the wind shifting from south-east to the opposite quarter, prevented their coming much nearer at that time. In the afternoon the Commodore again got under way, and came about a mile nearer Sullivan's Island.

Next morning, June 28, the following was the disposition of the ships-of-war: The *Friendship*, at the distance of about a mile-and-a-half from Sullivan's Island, covering the *Thunder*

Bomb, the *Solebay, Sphinx, Bristol, Active, Experiment, Acteon* and *Syren*. About half-an-hour past ten o'clock in the forenoon, the *Thunder* began throwing shells on Fort Sullivan, and the *Active, Bristol, Experiment* and *Solebay*, came boldly up to the attack, in the order their names are put down. A little before eleven o'clock, the garrison fired four or five shot at the *Active*, while under sail, some of which struck her. These she did not seem to regard till within about 350 yards of the Fort, when she dropped anchor and poured in a broadside. Her example was in a few minutes followed by the other three vessels, when there ensued one of the most heavy and incessant cannonades perhaps ever known. The bomb vessel [a ship equipped to fire mortar rounds] was at the same time throwing shells. A firing was heard from the advanced post at the north-east end of the Island, and more vessels were seen coming up. Our brave garrison (consisting of the 2d Regiment of Provincials, a Detachment of Artillery, and some Volunteers), under all these difficulties, which to the far greater part were entirely new, encouraged by the example of their gallant Commander, Col. William Moultrie, and the rest of the officers, behaved with the cool intrepidity of veterans. Our cannon were well served, and did dreadful execution. About twelve o'clock the *Sphinx*, *Acteon* and *Syren*, got entangled with a shoal, called the Middle Ground. The two first ran foul of each other; the *Sphinx* got off with the loss of her bowsprit, but the *Acteon* stuck fast. The *Syren* also got off. Much about the same time the bomb vessel ceased firing, after having thrown upwards of sixty shells. We have since learnt, that her beds got damaged, and that it will require much repairing before she is fit for service again. In the afternoon the enemy's fire was increased by that of the *Syren* and *Friendship*, which came within 500 yards of the Fort.

Till near seven o'clock was the enemy's fire kept up, without intermission. It slackened considerably after that, and they only returned the garrison's fire, but generally twenty-fold. At half after nine, the firing on both sides ceased, and, at eleven, the ships slipped their cables.

About the time the ships came up, an armed schooner and sloop came nearer our advanced post, in order to cover the landing of their troops, and every other preparation for that purpose was made—the soldiers even got into their boats, and a number of shell were thrown into our entrenchments, but did no other damage than wounding one soldier, notwithstanding which, they never once attempted to land. At the advanced post were stationed Col. [William] Thomson with his Rangers, some companies of Militia and a detachment of Artillery. They had one 18-pounder and two field pieces, from which they returned the enemy's fire. They were reinforced in the afternoon with Col. [Peter] Muhlenburg's Virginia Battalion.

Next morning all the men-of-war, except the *Acteon*, were retired about two miles from the island, which they had quietly effected under cloud of night. The garrison fired several shot at the *Acteon*, which she returned; but soon after her crew set her on fire, and abandoned her, leaving her colors flying, guns loaded, with all her ammunition, provisions and stores on board. They had not been long gone before several boats from the Island went to her. Lieut. Jacob Milligan, with some others, went on board, and brought off her [Union] Jack, bell, some sails and stores, while the flames were bursting out on all sides. He fired three of her guns at the Commodore. In less than half-an-hour after they quitted her, she blew up.

The *Bristol*, against which the fire was chiefly directed, is very much damaged. It is said that not less than seventy balls went through her. Her mizzen mast was so much hurt, that they have since replaced it with another. The main mast is cut away about fifteen feet below the hounds; and, instead of her broad pendant soaring on a lofty mast, it is now hardly to be seen on a jury main mast considerably lower than the fore mast. The *Experiment* had her mizzen gaff shot away; the other vessels sustained little damage in their rigging. The loss in the fleet, according to the report of the deserters, is about 180 killed and wounded; among the former is Captain Morrison, of the *Bristol*. Sir Peter Parker had the hind part of his breeches shot away, which laid his posteriors bare, and his knee pan hurt by a splinter. There have been several funerals in the fleet since the engagement; and from the parade of some, it is conjectured they were of officers of ranks. Some of the deserters say that Capt. Scott, of the *Experiment*, is among the killed.

The loss of the garrison was as follows:

> Artillery—Killed, 1 matross [gunner's mate]; wounded, 2 matrosses.
> 3d Regiment—Killed, 1 sergeant, 9 rank and file; wounded, Lieuts. Gray and Hall, the fife major, 1 sergeant, 19 rank and file.
> An officer's mulatto waiting boy was killed.
> Total Killed, 12; wounded, 23.

Both the officers were but slightly wounded, and are well[;] five of the wounded privates are since dead.

The works are very little damaged, but hardly a hut or tree on the island escaped the shot entirely. Many thousands of the enemy's shot have been picked up on the island.

General Lee was at Haddrel's Point at the beginning of

the action, and went in a boat, through a thick fire, to the fort, where he stayed some time. He says, in the whole course of his military service he never knew men behave better, and cannot sufficiently praise both officers and soldiers for their coolness and intrepidity. The behavior of two sergeants deserves to be remembered. In the beginning of the action, the flag-staff was shot away, which, being observed by Sergeant [William] Jasper, of the Grenadiers, he immediately jumped from one of the embrasures upon the beach, took up the flag, and fixed it on a sponge staff. With it in his hand he mounted the merlon, and notwithstanding the shot flew as thick as hail around him, he leisurely fixed it. Sergeant McDonald, of Capt. Huger's company, while exerting himself in a very distinguished manner, was cruelly shattered by a cannon ball. In a few minutes he expired, after having uttered these remarkable words: "My friends, I am dying; but don't let the cause of liberty expire with me." His comrades felt for him. The gallant Jasper immediately removed his mangled corpse from their sight, and cried aloud: "Let us revenge that brave man's death!" The day after the action, his Excellency, the President, presented Sergeant Jasper with a sword, as a mark of esteem for his distinguished valor.

We hear that the fort on Sullivan's Island will be in future called Fort Moultrie, in honor of the gallant officer who commanded there on the memorable 28th of June, 1776.

The men-of-war dropped down several miles further from the island a few days after. The carpenters in the fleet had sufficient employment in repairing the vessels. Several deserters came from both fleet and army, who all agreed we need not expect another visit at present, that it was talked that the two large ships would go to English harbor in Antigua to get refitted; the transports, with the troops, to proceed to New York, under convoy of some men-of-war, to join the grand army; and that two frigates would be left to cruise between North Carolina and Georgia.

On the 2d of July, Gen. Lee sent a flag to the enemy, with a proposal to exchange a prisoner for Col. Ethan Allen, who it was said was in the fleet. A present of some fresh meat and vegetables was sent at the same time. Gen. Clinton being at Long Island, an answer was not received till two days after, when he informed Gen. Lee that Col. Allen was not on board, and in return for his present, sent some porter, cheese, &c. Two engineers came in the boat, but as they were received at some distance from the fort, they were deprived of an opportunity of seeing what they were probably sent to observe.

A sloop from the West Indies, with gunpowder, &c., ran aground on the 5th, in coming into Stono Inlet. She, a few days afterwards, went to pieces, the cargo having been previously taken out.

A number of the enemy's transports went to Long Island about ten days after the repulse, and took on board all the troops on it and Goat Island. About the same time some of their frigates and armed vessels went over the bar; and, on the 14th, the *Bristol* made an attempt to go out, in which she failed, having struck on the bar. She succeeded in another attempt, four days after, and came to an anchor off the harbor.

The transports, with the *Solebay*, *Thunder*, *Friendship*, and some of the small armed vessels, sailed on the 20th, steering a southward course; they were afterwards seen standing to the eastward. On the same day a brigantine, having on board fifty soldiers and six sailors, got aground near Dewees' Inlet. She was left unobserved by the rest, and on the day afterwards was taken by an armed flat or floating battery, commanded by Lieut. Pickering. The brigantine could not be got off, and was, therefore, burnt. She was mounted with six 4-pounders. The soldiers threw their small arms overboard, on seeing the approach of the flat. Four of the crew escaped in their boat.

On the 25th, the *Experiment* went over the bar, her lower tier of guns being taken out. She came to an anchor near the Commodore, *Syren*, and three transports, lying off the harbor. A frigate, which had not been here before, came to the Commodore in the afternoon of the 25th. Next morning she sailed for the southward, and two days after the *Syren* followed her.

This forenoon the *Active*, *Sphynx*, and a large transport, being all of the enemy's vessels within the bar, went out, and with the *Bristol*, *Experiment*, three transports and a tender, stood out to sea, steering an E.N.E. course.

NOTES

[1]R. W. Gibbes, *Documentary History of the American Revolution*, vol. 3 (New York: D. Appleton & Co., 1857), 12–19.
[2]William S. Powell, *North Carolina: A History* (Chapel Hill: University of North Carolina Press, 1988), 63–64.
[3]John Buchanan, *The Road to Guilford Courthouse: The American Revolution in the Carolinas* (New York: John Wiley & Sons, 1997), 10.

PART II

Cornwallis Comes to Carolina
January — August 1780

The Siege of Charleston

From *Memoirs of the American Revolution*,[1]
by General William Moultrie

Until the end of the war—and quite possibly after—the British government believed that most Americans were still loyal to the Crown, and that if its army could only defeat George Washington and the Continental Army once and for all, their redcoats would be welcomed as liberators.[2] Washington, though he suffered defeats both minor and disastrous, proved too canny, too persistent, and too charismatic.

After four years in which the war was confined mostly to back-and-forth campaigning north of the Potomac, the British in 1779 decided again to attempt hitting the colonies where Washington wasn't, and planned another attack on Charleston.

The British gained a sudden and unexpected foothold in the South when they took Savannah on December 29, 1778. The attack was supposed to have been a raid only, but bold British action met with confused and lax defense, and Savannah was taken so quickly that "the town was scarcely damaged,"[3] according to historian John S. Pancake. In the fall of 1779, a combined force of soldiers from the French army, the Continental Army, and Carolina militia tried to retake Savannah, but it was beaten back by the veteran British defenders. The French sailed away, while the Americans retreated to Charleston.

A British fleet of troop transports and warships sailed from New York the day after Christmas 1779. As in 1776, General Sir Henry Clinton was in command, with Charles, Lord Cornwallis, his deputy. Storms scattered much of the fleet (one ship was driven all the way across the Atlantic to English shores[4]), so the British did not land in Savannah until February 1, 1780. After sending a detachment to Augusta as a diversion, the reassembled British fleet crept up the coast and began landing troops on what is now Seabrook Island, only 30 miles south of Charleston, on February 11.

Charleston's defense was in the hands of General Benjamin Lincoln of Massachusetts, commander of American forces in the Southern Department. Fat, lame, and narcoleptic, Lincoln was nonetheless liked and respected by most everyone who dealt with him, even the haughty rice kings. Before and after the war, Lincoln showed himself to be brave, decent, and humane: he commanded the troops that put down Shay's Rebellion, doing so with delicacy and recommending leniency to the captured leaders; rice kings who sent their sons to Harvard after the war asked Lincoln to watch out for them.[5] Despite Lincoln's fine qualities, his defense of Charleston was ineffective. After calls for reinforcements, he had about 5,000 troops with which to defend the city, yet he sent little more than skirmishers to face the British approaching overland. He was unable to convince or coerce the American naval commander to block the British warships approaching Charleston Harbor. The heroic 1776 defense of Sullivan's Island would not be repeated. Though strong fortifications protected the Charleston peninsula, British artillery—from both land and sea—was close enough to level the city, something the rice kings did not have the stomach to allow. By late March, the British were on the banks of the Ashley River, and Lincoln's 5,000 troops were trapped.

William Moultrie, the hero of Sullivan's Island, gave the following account of the siege and fall of Charleston. His memoirs consist mainly of his and others' correspondence, punctuated by recollections and observations such as the one that begins this excerpt. He also includes a journal of the siege written by a French engineer serving with the Continentals. Its brevity reveals the increasing desperation of the defenders of Charleston.

≈

The smallpox breaking out in Charlestown was a very good pretence for the militia not coming into town: in fact, they dreaded that disorder more than the enemy.

The British finding they could make no impression upon the northern states, reversed the proverb of "taking the bull by the horns," and turned their thoughts on the southern states; their late success in the repulse of the French and Americans from Savannah, and still keeping possession, encouraged them in the undertaking, and in December a large army embarked from New York, under command of Sir Henry Clinton, convoyed by Admiral [Mariot] Arbuthnot, with several men of war: they had a long and boisterous passage, and arrived at Savannah on the 11th of February; after staying there a few days, a strong detachment under General Patterson was ordered to cross over to Purisburgh, and march through the southern parts of the state; whilst Sir Henry Clinton with the body of the army, came round with the fleet to Stono Inlet, and landed the troops on John and James' Islands. We soon received accounts of the arrival of the British army in Savannah: at this time the legislature were sitting, they immediately adjourned, and all officers and soldiers were ordered to their posts....

A Journal of the Siege of Charlestown

Tuesday, March 28th, 1780
The enemy crossed Ashley River, in force, above the ferry.

Wednesday, 29th
The enemy advanced on the neck. The [American] light infantry were this evening reinforced with two companies, and the command given to Colonel [John] Laurens.

Thursday, 30th
The enemy came on, as far as Gibbs', where they continued skirmishing throughout the day, with our light infantry: the enemy were reinforced in the evening with two field pieces, and 90 men, which obliged our party to retire into garrison about dark. Captain Bowman of the North Carolina brigade

killed; Major [Edward] Hyrne, and seven privates wounded. The enemy were all this day transporting troops from Old Town, on Wappoo-neck, to Gibbs'.

Friday, 31st
The garrison employed in mounting cannon; throwing traverses, etc.

Saturday, April 1st
Nothing material: the troops employed as yesterday.

Sunday, 2nd
Last night the enemy broke ground, and this morning, appeared two redoubts; one nearly opposite the nine gun battery, on the right of the hornwork; and the other, a little to the left of the same, at about 1200 yards distance from our lines.

Monday, 3rd
The enemy employed in completing their two redoubts, and erecting one on our left, at an equal distance from the rest.

Tuesday, 4th
Several deserters within these three or four days . . . say the enemy on Thursday last had upwards of 20 men killed and wounded; among the latter, a lieutenant colonel of the 60th regiment; Lord St. Clair [wounded] badly; and that they are bringing their cannon on the neck: since the appearance of the enemy's works, they have been cannonaded: two ten-inch and one seven-inch mortars were removed from the Bay, and employed in retarding them. The enemy all this

day employed in finishing their redoubts, and throwing up a line of communication.

Wednesday, 5th
Last night the enemy continued their approaches to Hamstead Hill, on which they erected a battery for twelve cannon; and a mortar battery a little in the rear. The cannon and mortars employed as usual, in annoying their works: the battery from Wappoo, and the galleys, have thrown several shot into town; by which, one of the inhabitants of King Street was killed.

Thursday, 6th
The enemy approached from their center redoubt and erected a five-gun battery on the angle, between batteries no. 11 and 12. The Virginians, under Brigadier General [William] Woodford, got in by the way of Addison's Ferry; and some North Carolina militia under Colonel Harrington.

Friday, 7th
This afternoon twelve sail of the enemy's vessels passed Fort Moultrie, under a very heavy fire; one of them, supposed to be a store ship, having met with some accident, ran aground in the cove, where she was blown up by her own people: the remainder were ten square-rigged vessels; viz., one fifty and two forty-four gun ships; four frigates; two ships, supposed to be store ships; a schooner and sloop anchored under Fort Johnson.

Saturday, 8th
The enemy employed in finishing their batteries on the right.

Sunday, 9th

The enemy last night continued their approaches from their redoubt on the left, and threw up a battery for ten cannon, against the angle of our advanced redoubt, and the redan no. 7. Some shot were thrown at the shipping by our batteries in town, but without effect.

Monday, 10th

Sir Henry Clinton and Admiral Arbuthnot summoned the town.

Summons to Major General Lincoln
April 10th, 1780

Sir Henry Clinton, general and commander-in-chief of His Majesty's forces . . . and Vice Admiral Arbuthnot, commander-in-chief of His Majesty's ships in North America . . . regretting the effusion of blood, and consonant to humanity towards the town and garrison of Charlestown, of the havoc and desolation with which they are threatened from the formidable force surrounding them by land and sea. An alternative is offered at this hour to the inhabitants, of saving their lives and property contained in the town, or of abiding by the fatal consequences of a cannonade and storm.

Should the place in a fallacious security, or its commander in a wanton indifference to the fate of its inhabitants, delay the surrender, or should public stores or shipping be destroyed, the resentment of an exasperated soldiery may intervene; but the same mild and compassionate offer can never be renewed.

The respective commanders, who hereby summons the town, do not apprehend so rash a part, as further resistance will be taken, but rather that the gates will be opened, and themselves received with a degree of confidence which will forebode further reconciliation.

Henry Clinton,
M. Arbuthnot

From General Lincoln
Headquarters, Charlestown, April 10th, 1780

Gentlemen,

I have received your summons of this date; sixty days have passed since it has been known that your intentions against this town were hostile; in which, time has been offered to abandon it; but duty and inclination point to the propriety of supporting it to the last extremity.

I have the honor to be,
Your Excellency's humble servant,

B. Lincoln

Tuesday and Wednesday, 11th and 12th
The enemy [was] busied in completing their works and mounting their cannon.

Thursday, 13th
Between 9 and 10 o'clock this morning, the enemy opened their cannon and mortar batteries. The cannonade and bombardment continued, with short intermissions, until midnight: the galleys and battery at Wappoo also fired. An embrasure at redan no. 7 destroyed; a sergeant and private of the North Carolina brigade killed; a twenty-six pounder destroyed, and one eighteen pounder dismounted, in the flanking battery, on the right: some women and children killed in town. The enemy's cannon were chiefly twenty-four pounders; and their mortars from five-and-an-half to ten inches: they threw several carcasses [incendiary shells] from eight and ten inch mortars, by which two houses were burnt.

Friday, 14th
The enemy began an approach on the right, and kept up a fire of small arms. Cannonade and bombardment continued. One sergeant of the North Carolinians killed by a cannonball: one of the militia artillery killed, and one wounded: two matrosses [gunner's mates] of the South Carolina artillery killed.

Saturday, 15th
The enemy continued approaching on the right; the mortars ordered to the right, and commence a firing immediately, to annoy them. A continual fire of small arms, cannon, and mortars. A battery of two guns, opened by the enemy at Stiles'

place on James Island. Major [Thomas] Grimball's corps of militia relieved from the advance redoubt by a detachment of continental artillery, commanded by Major [Ephraim] Mitchell.

Sunday, 16th
It is said the enemy attempted to land at Hobcaw Neck with two gunboats, but were prevented by Colonel Malmadie [Marquis Francis de Malmedy]. Two 18-pounders, a quantity of provisions, and other valuable articles got out of the wreck of the vessel near Fort Moultrie.

Monday, 17th
A man, inhabitant of the town, killed by a cannonball, and a woman wounded; both from Wappoo battery.

Tuesday, 18th
The enemy continued a warm firing from their cannon, mortars, and small arms. Mr. [Philip] Neyle, aide-de-camp to General Moultrie, killed by a cannonball. We advanced a breastwork to the left of the square redoubt, for riflemen, to annoy the enemy on their approach. Five men killed by small arms, and three wounded by a shell; a sentinel at the abatis had his arm shot off by one of our own cannon; a twelve pounder bursted in the hornwork, by which two men were much hurt. The enemy ceased throwing large shells. We hear that our cavalry under General [Isaac] Huger have been defeated, and that we lost between 20 or 30 killed and wounded; among the former was Major [Paul] Vernier of Pulaski's Legion. General [Charles] Scott with the light infantry crossed Cooper River

into town; about 40 Virginians got in last night. The enemy continued their approaches to the right, within 250 yards of the front of the square redoubt; they threw during the night a great number of shells from 16 royals and Cohorns [cannon], chiefly in the North Carolina camp: one man killed, and two wounded.

Wednesday, 19th
The enemy began an approach from the left battery, towards our advanced redoubt; and moved some mortars into the former: they also advanced on Hobcaw Neck, and exchanged a few shot with our advance party. Two or three persons killed in town.

Thursday, 20th
The approaches continued on the left; their mortars removed from their left battery, into their approaches; an eighteen pounder dismounted at Captain Bottard's battery on the right; four of their galleys, after dark, moved from Wappoo Creek to the shipping at Fort Johnson, under a very heavy fire from our batteries. The enemy retreated from Hobcaw across Wappataw Bridge, which it is said they have burnt. Two magazines in the batteries commanded by Captain Sisk blew up by shells, but no persons hurt.

Friday, 21st
A flag sent to Sir Henry Clinton.

Charlestown, April 21st, 1780

Sir,

I am willing to enter into the consideration of terms of capitulation, if such can be obtained as are honorable to the army, and safe for the inhabitants. I have to propose a cessation of hostilities for six hours, for the purpose of digesting such articles.

> I have the honor to be,
> Your Excellency's, &c.

> B. Lincoln

NOTES

[1] William Moultrie, *Memoirs of the American Revolution, So Far As It Related to the States of North and South-Carolina, and Georgia*, vol. 2 (New York: David Longworth, 1802), 44–73.

[2] John S. Pancake, *This Destructive War: The British Campaign in the Carolinas, 1780–1782* (Tuscaloosa: University of Alabama Press, 1985), 13.

[3] Ibid., 32.

[4] John Buchanan, *The Road to Guilford Courthouse: The American Revolution in the Carolinas* (New York: John Wiley & Sons, 1997), 27.

[5] Ibid, 48–49.

Buford's Quarter

From *A History of the Campaigns of 1780 and 1781*
in the Southern Provinces of North America,[1]
by Banastre Tarleton

Years after the American Revolution, when Banastre Tarleton was, according to John Buchanan, "the most famous British cavalryman of his day," he often contributed to political rallies by removing the glove that concealed his maimed hand—two of whose fingers he had left in the Carolinas—so he could show his disfigurement and yell, "For King and Country!"[2]

Tarleton may not have been a great political thinker, but he was probably not the sadist or psychopath he became in American legend. Most likely, he was simply a bullyboy, reckless, cruel, and unreflective; unlike most bullies, though, Tarleton was also brave, even dashing. Had he been born a Virginian—or had the British won—Tarleton would have become as romantic a figure as Light

Horse Harry Lee; had he been born in a different era, Tarleton could have been an exemplary Klansman, or an active member of certain college fraternities.

The son of a well-to-do Liverpool merchant who traded in sugar and slaves, Tarleton was only in his mid-20s during the British campaign in the Carolinas. In less than four years, he rose from cornet (or cavalry flag bearer) to lieutenant colonel and commander of the British Legion. The legion was a regiment combining infantry and cavalry, all of whom were Tories from Pennsylvania and New York. Tarleton and a few of his officers were the only British soldiers in the British Legion.[3]

Shortly after Benjamin Lincoln surrendered Charleston and its garrison, Sir Henry Clinton handed over his command to Charles, Lord Cornwallis (see "A Narrative of the Battle of Camden," pages 101-16) and returned to his headquarters in New York. Clinton had charged Cornwallis with establishing posts across South Carolina to keep the state firmly under British control. In May, Cornwallis and 2,500 troops left Charleston bound for the backcountry trading town of Camden. Ten days' march ahead of him was Colonel Abraham Buford and the remnants of the Continental Army in South Carolina. Knowing he would be unable to catch Buford with the bulk of his force, Cornwallis unleashed Tarleton.

Before the surrender of Charleston, Tarleton had begun to establish his reputation as a daring, effective, and lightning-fast commander. He had twice surprised and routed Continental cavalry under Colonel William Washington (a cousin of George, and an adversary Tarleton would meet again), once at Moncks Corner and again at Leneuds Ferry on the Santee River. Tarleton and his legion had also begun to establish a reputation for brutality. A French cavalryman who asked for quarter at Moncks Corner was instead hacked with sabers and left to die; after the battle, several dragoons entered the nearby plantation of a prominent Tory and assaulted the women gathered there. Cornwallis felt it necessary to write a letter to Tarleton reminding him that his responsibility for his troops did not end with the battle itself.[4]

Far behind, and outnumbered by, his quarry, Tarleton threw his men into pursuit. Tarleton in pursuit was relentless. Buford's destination was Hillsborough, North Carolina. He made it only to the area known as the Waxhaws, on the border between North and South Carolina, before Tarleton caught him. Buford ordered his men into formation and awaited the legion's attack.

Tarleton was a celebrity, a favorite of the Prince of Wales, when he wrote the following account of what happened next. He was largely accurate in his assessment of the battle itself, but he also attempted to explain, if not excuse, the behavior of his American-born troops after their American opponents surrendered. It was this behavior that would turn "Buford's quarter" into a rallying cry for the rebels, and Banastre Tarleton into "Bloody Ban."

Colonel Buford was among those who escaped on horseback.

~

On the 22nd, the army moved forwards upon the same road by which Colonel Buford had retreated 10 days before: The infantry marched to Nelson's ferry with as much expedition as the climate would allow. From this place, Earl Cornwallis thought proper to detach a corps, consisting of 40 of the 17th dragoons, and 130 of the Legion, with 100 mounted infantry of the same regiment, and a three-pounder, to pursue the Americans, who were now so much advanced, as to render any approach of the main body impracticable. Lieutenant

Colonel Tarleton, on this occasion, was desired to consult his own judgment, as to the distance of the pursuit, or the mode of attack: To defeat Colonel Buford, and to take his cannon, would undoubtedly, in the present state of the Carolinas, have considerable effect; but the practicability of the design appeared so doubtful, and the distance of the enemy so great, that the attempt could only be guided by discretional powers, and not by any antecedent commands. The detachment left the army on the 27th, and followed the Americans without any thing material happening on the route, except the loss of a number of horses, in consequence of the rapidity of the march, and the heat of the climate: By pressing horses on the road, the light troops arrived the next day at Camden, where Lieutenant Colonel Tarleton gained intelligence that Colonel Buford had quitted Rugeley's mills on the 26th, and that he was marching with great diligence to join a corps then upon the road from Salisbury to Charlotte town in North Carolina.

This information strongly manifested that no time was to be lost, and that a vigorous effort was the only resource to prevent the junction of the two American corps. At two o'clock in the morning, the British troops, being tolerably refreshed, continued their pursuit: They reached Rugeley's by daylight, where they learned that the Continentals were retreating above 20 miles in their front, towards the Catawba settlement, to meet their reinforcement. At this point, Tarleton might have contented himself with following them at his leisure to the boundary line of South Carolina, and from thence have returned upon his footsteps to join the main army, satisfied with pursuing the troops of Congress out of the province; but animated by the alacrity which he discovered both in the officers and men, to undergo all hardships, he put his detachment in motion, after adopting a stratagem to delay the march of the enemy: Captain [David] Kinlock, of the Legion, was employed to carry a summons to the American commander, which, by magnifying the number of the British, might intimidate him into submission, or at least delay him whilst he deliberated on an answer. Colonel Buford, after detaining the flag for some time, without halting his march, returned a defiance. By this time many of the British cavalry and mounted infantry were totally worn out, and dropped successively into the rear; the horses of the three-pounder were likewise unable to proceed. In this dilemma, Lieutenant Colonel Tarleton found himself not far distant from the enemy, and, though not in a suitable condition for action, he determined as soon as possible to attack, there being no other expedient to stop their progress, and prevent their being reinforced the next morning: The only circumstance favorable to the British light troops at this hour, was the known inferiority of the Continental cavalry, who could not harass their retreat to Earl Cornwallis's army, in case they were repulsed by the infantry.

At three o'clock in the afternoon, on the confines of South Carolina, the advanced guard of the British charged a sergeant and four men of the American light dragoons, and made them prisoners in the rear of their infantry. This event happening under the eyes of the two commanders, they respectively prepared their troops for action. Colonel Buford's force consisted of 380 Continental infantry of the Virginia line, a detachment of [William] Washington's cavalry, and two six-pounders: He chose his post in an open wood, to the right of the road; he formed his infantry in one line, with a small reserve; he placed his colors in the center; and he ordered his cannon, baggage, and wagons to continue their march.

Lieutenant Colonel Tarleton made his arrangement for the attack with all possible expedition: He confided his right wing, which was composed of 60 dragoons, and nearly as many mounted infantry, to Major [Charles] Cochrane, desiring him to dismount the latter, to gall the enemy's flank, before he moved against their front with his cavalry: Captains Corbet and Kinlock were directed, with the 17th dragoons and part of the Legion, to charge the center of the Americans; whilst Lieutenant Colonel Tarleton, with 30 chosen horse and some infantry, assaulted their right flank and reserve: This particular situation the commanding officer selected for himself, that he might discover the effect of the other attacks. The dragoons, the mounted infantry, and the three-pounder in the rear, as they could come up with their tired horses, were ordered to form something like a reserve, opposite to the enemy's center, upon a small eminence that commanded the road; which disposition afforded the British light troops an object to rally to, in case of a repulse, and made no inconsiderable impression on the minds of their opponents.

This disposition being completed without any fire from the enemy, though within 300 yards of their front, the cavalry advanced to the charge. On their arrival within 50 paces, the Continental infantry presented, when Tarleton was surprised to hear their officers command them to retain their fire till the British cavalry were nearer. This forbearance in not firing before the dragoons were within 10 yards of the object of their attack prevented their falling into confusion on the charge, and likewise deprived the Americans of the farther use of their ammunition: Some officers, men, and horses suffered by this fire; but the battalion was totally broken, and slaughter was commenced before Lieutenant Colonel Tarleton could remount another horse, the one with which he led his dragoons being overturned by the volley. Thus in a few minutes ended an affair which might have had a very different termination. The British troops had two officers killed, one wounded; three privates killed, 13 wounded; and 31 horses killed and wounded. The loss of officers and men was great on the part of the Americans, owing to the dragoons so effectually breaking the infantry, and to a report amongst the cavalry that they had lost their commanding officer, which stimulated the soldiers to a vindictive asperity not easily restrained. Upwards of 100 officers and men were killed on the spot; three colors, two six-pounders, and above 100 prisoners, with a number of wagons, containing two royals [cannon], quantities of new clothing, other military stores, and camp equipage, fell into the possession of the victors.

NOTES

[1] Banastre Tarleton, *A History of the Campaigns of 1780 and 1781 in the Southern Provinces of North America* (Dublin: printed for Colles, Exshaw, White, H. Whitestone, Burton, etc., 1787), 27–31.

[2] John Buchanan, *The Road to Guilford Courthouse: The American Revolution in the Carolinas* (New York: John Wiley & Sons, 1997), 58.

[3] What made a person British or American, in the context of the Revolutionary War, is a contentious subject. Many natives of the American colonies, before and after the Declaration of Independence,

considered themselves British; many "American" officers and soldiers, notably Continental general Charles Lee and partisan leader William Richardson Davie, were born in the United Kingdom.

[4]Buchanan, *The Road to Guilford Courthouse*, 68.

Moffitt's Minute Men

From *Autobiography of a
Revolutionary Soldier,*[1]
by James Collins

*The worst of the Revolutionary War in the Carolinas did
not come from Charleston's fall or Tarleton's cruelties. The worst
came from the partisan bands, Tory and rebel alike, who waged
a simmering, savage war against each other both before and after
Cornwallis's campaign. Cornwallis's year in the Carolinas, though,
caused the partisan war to boil over, as Tories were emboldened
by the British success and rebels found themselves the last line of
defense against complete subjugation.*

*The Whig victory at the Great Cane Break had eliminated
the Tories as a serious threat to the Provincial Congress's rule in
South Carolina, but it did not pacify the back country for long. As*

they had during the Regulator movement, communities began to organize partisan bands to protect themselves and the side they had chosen.

Many of the leaders of partisan bands would become legends in the Carolinas, if not the nation: Francis Marion, Thomas Sumter, Andrew Pickens, William R. Davie, Isaac Shelby. After the war, grateful citizens would name counties and towns after them.

Much of the war in the back country, though, was fought by leaders whose names were soon forgotten. They led fewer men, participated in less significant battles, or simply lacked talented chroniclers to spread their fame. But these rebel partisans had the same effect as Sumter and Marion, although perhaps on a smaller scale: they kept the Tories at bay, and after the British launched their reconquest of the Carolinas, they kept British flanks and supply lines constantly harassed, never allowing Cornwallis the security that would let him throw the full force of his army against the Continentals. They kept the British busy until the Continental Army in the South could again be an effective fighting force, and maybe find effective generals to lead it.

James Collins was a teenager living on the family farm in what is now York County, South Carolina, when he agreed to be a scout for one such rebel band. He would end up seeing much more action than he intended. His autobiography is a vivid and highly personal account of what he saw. In this excerpt, he describes how he and his father became partisans, an experience that was replicated by hundreds of men across the Carolina back country.

~

I began to grow up—times began to be troublesome, and people began to divide into parties. Those that had been good friends in times past, became enemies; they began to watch each other with jealous eyes, and were designated by the names of Whig and Tory. Recruiting officers were out in all directions, to enlist soldiers. My brother, older than myself, enlisted, and went off to the army. My father remonstrated against it but in vain. There was a Mr. Moffitt in the neighborhood who was then captain of the militia, was pretty shrewd and an active partisan. I had often been sent on business, by my father, in various directions through the country, and was frequently employed by others to hunt stray horses, etc., consequently I became acquainted with all the by-paths for 20 or 30 miles around. Moffitt consulted with my father and it was agreed that I should be made use of merely as a collector of news. In order to prepare me for business, I had to receive several lectures. I was furnished with documents—sometimes a list of several stray horses with marks and brands, sometimes with papers and other business. I was to attend all public places, make . . . inquiry only about the business I was sent on, and pay strict attention to all that was passing in conversation and otherwise. I succeeded for some time without incurring the least suspicion, by which means the Tories were several time[s] disappointed in their plans without being able to account for the cause.

There existed at that time at least three classes of Whigs, and three of Tories. The first class of Whigs were those who determined to fight it out to the last, let the consequence be what it might; the second class were those who would fight a little when the wind was favorable, but so soon as it shifted to an unfavorable point would draw back and give up all for lost; the third class were those who were favorable to the cause, provided it prospered and they could enjoy the benefit but would not risk one hair of their heads to attain it.

There was a class of Tories who I believe were Tories from principle; another class believed it impossible for the cause of liberty to succeed, and thought in the end, whatever they got, they would be enabled to hold, and so become rich—they resorted to murdering and plunder, and every means to get hold of property; another class were Tories entirely through fear, and fit for nothing only to be made tools of by the others, and all cowards too.

There was another class of men amongst us, who pretended neutrality entirely on both sides; they pretended friendship to all, and prayed, "Good God! Good Devil!" not knowing into whose hands they might fall. Of these last there were several in the neighborhood, and by some means, some one or more became acquainted with the part I had acted; it became known to the Tories by the same means. They swore revenge. By some of the same people this was communicated to me, and I was cautioned of the danger that awaited me. It was also communicated to my father, and he advised me not to act in that part any longer, else I would suffer the penalty if caught. I took some alarm, and proposed enlisting in order to avoid danger. My father counseled me otherwise; he said the time was at hand when volunteers would be called for, and by joining them I would be equally safe; if I went to battle I stood as fair a chance; besides, I would be less exposed, less fatigued, and if there should be any time of resting, I could come home and enjoy it; he said he had had some experience and learned a lesson from that.[2]

The British and Tories had overrun Georgia, and even

driven out the celebrated [Colonel Elijah] Clarke, with all his veterans, as far as the very confines of North Carolina. All the south and southwestern parts of South Carolina were nearly subjugated, and but a small part stood out with firmness, and that part itself divided. The British were pressing on Charleston, and had eventually got possession of it, and now began to come "squally times." So soon as Charleston fell, there was a proclamation for all to come forward, submit, and take protection; peace and pardon should be granted. In order to expedite the business, there were officers sent out in various directions, with guards or companies of men, to receive the submission of the people. Vast numbers flocked in and submitted; some through fear, some through willingness, and others, perhaps, through a hope that all things would settle down and war cease. But not so; there was some conditions annexed,[3] that some of the patriots of the day could not submit to and therefore determined to hold out a little longer. Among the officers sent out on this occasion, there was one Lord Huck, who came up and stationed himself at or near Fishing Creek at some distance below where we lived. His proclamation came out and a day was appointed to deliver his speeches. Almost all the men of families attended. He got up, harangued the people in a very rough and insulting manner and submitted his propositions for their acceptance. Some bowed to his scepter, but far the greater part returned home without submitting.

I omitted to mention in the proper place, that in conversation with my father on the subject of enlistment, he observed to me that should volunteers be called, which he confidently anticipated, then he would join the ranks; he said, "Though over age for the laws of my country to demand it, yet I think the nature of the case requires the best energies of every man who is a friend to liberty." Not many miles distant from where this Lord Huck, whom I have mentioned, had made his stand, there was a set of ironworks called Billy Hill's Ironworks [see "Huck's Defeat," pages 89-94], which were very profitable, both to the proprietor and all the country around. Lord Huck, provoked at the non-compliance of the people, determined to take vengeance; and to that end mustered his forces, charged on the ironworks, killed several men, set the works on fire, and reduced them to ashes. I must here relate the expression of my father, when he returned home from Lord Huck's exhibition. My stepmother asked him thus: "Well, Daniel, what news?" My father replied, "Nothing very pleasant. I have come home determined to take my gun and when I lay it down, I lay down my life with it." Then turning to me said, "My son you may prepare for the worst; the thing is fairly at issue. We must submit and become slaves, or fight. For my part I am determined— tomorrow I will go and join Moffitt."

Moffitt, while these things were transpiring, had been engaged in raising volunteers, to be all mounted and ready at a minute's warning, to be called "Minute Men." He had already raised about 70 men. A nomination of officers had taken place, and he was unanimously chosen colonel of the troops. Accordingly, next day we shouldered our guns and went to Moffitt. The gun that I had to take was what was called a blue barrel shotgun. When we presented ourselves, "Well," said the colonel to my father, "Daniel, I suppose you intend to fight." My father said he had come to that conclusion.

"Well, James," he said to me, "we shall have plenty for you to do, and two or three more such, if they could all have as good luck as you. We will try to take care of you and not let the Tories catch you."

Notes

[1] James Potter Collins, *Autobiography of a Revolutionary Soldier*, revised and prepared by John M. Roberts (Clinton, La.: *Feliciana Democrat*, 1859), 22–25.

[2] Collins's father had served in the French and Indian War, Collins says elsewhere in his autobiography.

[3] Many of the Carolinas' most celebrated rebel partisans, including Andrew Pickens and Thomas Sumter, surrendered to the British after the fall of Charleston and quietly retired to their homes as parolees. They returned to the field only after Sir Henry Clinton abrogated the terms of surrender and required all adult males to swear allegiance to the king, which would further require healthy men to take up arms against rebels, if so called.

The Battle of Ramsour's Mill

From *The Revolutionary War Sketches of William R. Davie*[1]

After the surrender of General Benjamin Lincoln and his men in Charleston and the massacre of Colonel Abraham Buford's men in the Waxhaws, Carolina Tories were jubilant in anticipation of relief from Whig rule. Following the British call for aid from loyalists, Lieutenant Colonel John Moore left Cornwallis's army for home to organize a Tory militia in what is now Lincoln County, North Carolina (named for Benjamin Lincoln). By mid-June, more than 1,000 loyalists had gathered at Ramsour's Mill in what is now Lincolnton.

The commanding officer of rebel militia in western North Carolina, Brigadier General Griffith Rutherford, was at his camp in Charlotte when he heard about the gathering. Rutherford immediately sent orders to Colonel Francis Locke in what is now Catawba County to take his force of 400 militia toward Ramsour's Mill, where he would rendezvous with Rutherford and his troops. The two officers missed their rendezvous point, however, and Locke reached the area on June 20, ahead of Rutherford. He found that though the loyalists had more men, many of them were old, young, or unarmed. At dawn, Locke launched a surprise attack on the Tory camp.

Historian John Buchanan wrote of Ramsour's Mill that "to call the fight there a battle would lend it a formality it did not possess. It was a clash of two armed mobs. Toward the end the fighting resembled an old-fashioned Pier 6 brawl between longshoremen and strikebreakers."[2] Locke's militia charged uphill into the Tory camp; the Tories quickly rallied, and the fighting was done at close quarters, often hand to hand. As in many clashes during the Revolutionary War in the Carolinas, brother fought brother, neighbor fought neighbor, and American fought American. In the end, the rebels swept the Tories from their camp, though many of the Tories regrouped across a nearby creek. Locke, seeing that casualties and "scattering" had left him only 110 members of his force, dispatched two officers to find Rutherford and urge him to hurry to Ramsour's Mill. Rutherford, still seven miles from the mill when he met these riders, sent ahead a reinforcement of 65 dragoons under Major William Richardson Davie.

Davie, one of the few British-born participants at Ramsour's Mill, arrived too late for the actual fighting. Born in Yorkshire in 1756, he had moved with his parents to America in 1764. They settled in the Waxhaws. While Davie was an undergraduate at the College of New Jersey (now Princeton University) in 1776, he and some classmates organized a volunteer company of students and marched to Elizabethtown, New Jersey, to join Washington's Continentals. After graduation, Davie studied law in Salisbury,

North Carolina, but kept interrupting his studies to aid in the Whig cause. In 1779, he organized his own cavalry force and received a lieutenant's commission from North Carolina governor Richard Caswell. A year before the fight at Ramsour's Mill, Davie was seriously wounded while leading a charge against a British expedition from Savannah that had reached the outskirts of Charleston. After recovering at home, Davie was reinstated as a major and again raised his own troop of cavalry, a partisan band he would command with unrivaled success.[3]

Davie was later described as "a tall, elegant man in his person, graceful and commanding in his manners."[4] Among the many he impressed in his long public career was another Waxhaws boy, Andrew Jackson, who served briefly with Davie's partisans as a scout. Jackson, whose father had died either before or just after Andrew was born, and who would lose the rest of his family before the end of the war, used Davie as his role model of an officer and a gentleman for the rest of his life.[5]

After the war, Davie served as one of North Carolina's delegates to the Constitutional Convention, as governor of the state, and as President John Adams's special envoy to France during Napoleon's reign. But he perhaps made his greatest impact as a state legislator, when he introduced a bill to charter the University of North Carolina and spearheaded the creation of the first public university in the United States.

Though he arrived too late for the battle, Davie left the following account of what happened at Ramsour's Mill, and the circumstances that led to the fight.

≈

The surrender of Charleston and the defeat of Buford's

detachment completed the conquest of South Carolina, the people generally submitted either personally or by a deputation of commissioners; but as this was well known to be the effect of panic, and that benumbing stupor consequent on such an impression, the upper country was carefully reconnoitered, the minds and principles of the inhabitants examined, and the proper places fixed upon to establish posts that might keep the country in awe, and further subjection; with these views the enemy in the month of June had established strong advance posts at the Hanging Rock and Rocky Mount [in South Carolina; see "The Gamecock," pages 95-100]; these positions were well chosen, they were capable of supporting each other and not only entirely covered the northern part of that state, but encouraged the Loyalists in North Carolina to assemble in large bodies, and make considerable attempts to establish themselves, in different parts of the country. About this time a certain Colonel Moore collected 1100 of the disaffected at Ramsour's mill on the west side of the Catawba River, and Colonel [Samuel] Bryan was at the same time secretly assembling a large body in the Forks of the Yadkin; numbers embodied in small parties near the South Carolina line, and being acquainted with the country carried their depredations in every direction. The militia were everywhere in arms, but every place wanted protection; at length about [300] men [comprised of the militia of Burke, Lincoln, and Rowan counties] assembled under Colonel Francis Lock and 700 under General Rutherford including the South Carolina refugees, under Colonel [Thomas] Sumter, [William] Neale and others, and some cavalry under Major Davie who had a commission to raise an independent corps [near Charlotte]. It was agreed to attack

Moore's camp at Ramsour's as the most dangerous body of the enemy, on the 22nd following; for this purpose Colonel Lock marched to cross the river at Sherrill's and Beattie's fords while General Rutherford also moved to cross below at Tuckaseegee ford. These divisions were to have met in the night near the enemy and [to have attacked] them at the break of day, but the march of both parties was too circuitous, and the point of rendezvous too distant to ensure punctuality; General Rutherford did not arrive, and Colonel Lock, who had gained his position early in the night, called a council of the officers in which they resolved to attack the enemy notwithstanding the disparity of numbers. The Tories [were] encamped on a high ridge, clear of under wood, and covered with large oaks; their rear was protected by a millpond and their right flank by a strong fence. At day break the regiment advanced by companies; the enemy drew up behind the trees and baggage and the action became in a moment general; the enemy's fire was well directed, but the militia pressed forward with great spirit and intrepidity and in about 30 minutes the Loyalists gave way on all sides. The loss of the militia was heavy in officers.... A considerable number of the enemy were killed and wounded and they lost all their baggage.

The General arrived about an hour after the action and dispatched Major Davie with his cavalry in pursuit of the fugitives with orders to clear that part of the country of all straggling parties; many came and surrendered voluntarily, a great number were taken prisoners, some flying to South Carolina, others at their plantations, and in a few days that district of country lying between the river, the mountains, and their [South Carolina] line was entirely cleared of the enemy.

NOTES

[1] Blackwell P. Robinson, ed., *The Revolutionary War Sketches of William R. Davie* (Raleigh: North Carolina Department of Cultural Resources, Division of Archives and History, 1976), 7.

[2] John Buchanan, *The Road to Guilford Courthouse: The American Revolution in the Carolinas* (New York: John Wiley & Sons, 1997), 106.

[3] R. Neil Fulghum, *William Richardson Davie: Soldier, Statesman, and Founder of the University of North Carolina* (Chapel Hill: University of North Carolina, 2006), 4–5.

[4] Ibid., back cover.

[5] John Buchanan, *Jackson's Way: Andrew Jackson and the People of the Western Waters* (New York: John Wiley & Sons, 2001), 4.

The Battle at Stallions

From *The Memoir of Major Thomas Young*[1]

When Thomas Young was 16 years old, he joined a local partisan band operating around his home in what is now Union County, South Carolina. Only a few days later, in July 1780, he took part in his first skirmish, another of the short but savage clashes that defined the war in the back country and set brother against brother.

≈

I was born in Laurens District, S.C., on the seventeenth of January 1764. My father, Thomas Young, soon after removed to Union District where I have lived to this day.

In the spring of 1780, I think in April, Colonel [Thomas] Brandon was encamped with a party of 70 or 80 Whigs, about five miles below Union courthouse, where Christopher Young now lives. Their object was to collect forces for the approaching campaign, and to keep a check upon the Tories. They had taken prisoner one Adam Steedham, as vile a Tory as ever lived. By some means Steedham escaped during the night, and notified the Tories of Brandon's position. The Whigs were attacked by a large body of the enemy before day and completely routed. On that occasion, my brother, John Young, was murdered. I shall never forget my feelings when told of his death. I do not believe I had ever used an oath before that day, but then I tore open my bosom, and swore that I would never rest till I had avenged his death. Subsequently a hundred Tories felt the weight of my arm for the deed, and around Steedham's neck I fastened the rope as a reward for his cruelties. On the next day I left home in my shirt sleeves, and joined Brandon's party. Christopher Brandon and I joined at the same time, and the first engagement we were in, was at Stallions in York District.

We had received intelligence of a party of Tories, then stationed at Stallions; a detachment of about 50 Whigs under Colonel Brandon moved to attack them. Before we arrived at the house in which they were fortified, we were divided into two parties. Captain Love with a party of 16—of whom I was one—marched to attack the front, while Colonel Brandon, with the remainder, made a circuit to intercept those who should attempt to escape, and also to attack the rear. Mrs. Stallions was a sister of Captain Love, and on the approach of her brother she ran out, and begged him not to fire upon the house. He told her it was too late now, and that their only chance for safety was to surrender. She ran back to the house and sprang upon the door step, which was pretty high. At this moment, the house was attacked in the rear by Colonel

Brandon's party, and Mrs. Stallions was killed by a ball shot through the opposite door. At the same moment with Brandon's attack, our party raised a shout and rushed forward. We fired several rounds, which were briskly returned. It was not long, however, before the Tories ran up a flag, first upon the end of a gun, but as that did not look exactly peaceful, a ball was put through the fellow's arm, and in a few moments it was raised on a ram-rod, and we ceased firing.

While we were fighting a man was seen running through an open field near us. I raised my gun to shoot him, when some of our party exclaimed, "Don't fire; he is one of our own men." I drew down my gun, and in a moment he halted, wheeled round, and fired at us. Old Squire Kennedy (who was an excellent marksman) raised his rifle and brought him down. We had but one wounded, William Kennedy, who was shot by my side. I was attempting to fire in at the door of the house, when I saw two of the Tories in the act of shooting at myself and Kennedy. I sprang aside and escaped, calling at the same time to my companion, but he was shot (while moving) through the wrist and thigh. The loss of the Tories was two killed, four wounded, and 28 prisoners whom we sent to Charlotte, N.C. After the fight, Love and Stallions met and shed bitter tears; Stallions was dismissed on parole to bury his wife and arrange his affairs.

Notes

[1]Thomas Young, *The Memoir of Major Thomas Young* (Penfield, Ga.: *Orion* magazine, 1843).

Huck's Defeat

From Colonel William Hill's Memoirs of the Revolution[1]

William "Billy" Hill, a native of Northern Ireland by way of Pennsylvania, moved in 1762 to South Carolina's New Acquisition District, acquired in a border settlement with North Carolina. A few years later, Hill discovered iron ore on his property. By the time of the Revolutionary War, he was operating a mine and an ironworks.

In June 1780, as more and more men in the back country became rebel partisans, George Turnbull, the commander of the British post at Rocky Mount, South Carolina, sent Captain Christian Huck into the Catawba River Valley near the North Carolina–South Carolina line to quell the incipient insurrection. Huck was a Philadelphia Quaker and an attorney who had become a captain in Tarleton's British Legion—and a poor choice for such a mission. He made no attempt to hide his contempt for the rebels and back-country settlers in general, and his outrages against Whigs, their families, and their property proved to be one of the best recruiting tools the partisans had. Among Huck's affronts was the burning of Billy Hill's ironworks and home.

When Huck threatened the family of 27-year-old colonel William Bratton, he finally went too far. Though already attached to General Thomas Sumter (see "The Gamecock," pages 95-100), Bratton, Hill, John Moffitt, and other partisan leaders left Sumter's camp on the Catawba River to hunt down Huck and his mixed force of British Legion troops and loyalist militia. They found him camped at Williamson's plantation, not far from Bratton's home, on July 12, the same day as the fight at Stallions (see "The Battle at Stallions," pages 86-88).

Huck's Defeat was the first rebel victory over regular British troops (as opposed to Tory militia) since the fall of Charleston. It could have served as a warning to Cornwallis that the partisans were not to be underestimated. Fortunately for the American cause, the British did not heed the warning.

~

Here your Author wishes to remark that he by no means wishes to arrogate [claim] any thing to himself or to have it be supposed that he had or possessed more public virtue or firmness than other men who acted differently. And after these things took place the men appeared very anxious to keep in a body but they had no officers. I then advised them to ballot for two colonels and they did so and it appeared their choice fell upon a young man by the name of (Andrew) Neel and your Author; we then proceeded to further arrangements and that was for the men to choose all other of their officers, to form into companies, etc., we then formed a camp and erected the American standard. And as soon as this was known there were men both of the states of Georgia and South Carolina adding daily to our numbers that we soon became a respectable body and a few days after these things happened we received information that there was a Tory colonel by the name of [Matthew] Floyd in the western part of the District who much distressed the inhabitants and was collecting men to go to the British post at Rocky Mount. Upon this Colonel Neel with all the men but about 12 or 15 that was left to keep the camp went in pursuit of that party of Tories but unfortunately before he got to their settlement they had marched to Rocky Mount. And from there a certain Captain Huck with a company of horse and about 500 Tories came to the iron works, destroyed all the property they could not carry away, burned the forge furnace, grist and saw mills together with all other buildings even to the Negro huts, and bore away about 90 Negroes, all which was done before Colonel Neel returned with the army to camp. About this time I was informed that Colonel Sumter was then in Salisbury with a few men waiting for a reinforcement. I then wrote to him, informing him of our situation and that there was a probability of our making a handsome stand—and that we were about to form a junction with General [Griffith] Rutherford in North Carolina, that we were going to attack a large body of Tories that had collected at a place called Ramsour's Mill [see "The Battle of Ramsour's Mill," pages 80-85]. But so it was that a detached party of about 300 horse from General Rutherford attacked the Tory camp, said to be upwards of 1000 men, killed and dispersed the whole—and then it was that Colonel Sumter met with us from South Carolina. He then got authority from the civil and military authority of that State to impress or take wagons, horses, provisions of all kinds, from the enemy that was in that action—and to give a receipt to that state for the same. This being done we returned to South Carolina and formed a camp on the east side of the Catawba River at the place called Clem's Branch. From this [point] out all our proceedings of importance was done by a convention of the whole—a commission of captains appointed to take notice of all the property taken either from the enemy or friends, and a commissioner to supply us with provisions, etc.

After we had been some time at this camp as before mentioned, in order to prepare for actual service a number of men together with your author, being desirous to go into their own settlement on the west side of the river, in order to get a reinforce as well as other necessaries to enable us to keep the field—shortly after we crossed the river we were informed by our friends that Captain Huck, the same that had a few weeks before destroyed the iron works, had sent to most of the houses in the settlement to notify the aged men, the young being in camp, to meet him at a certain place, that he desired to make terms with them, and that he would put them in the King's peace. Accordingly they met him, he undertook to harangue them on the certainty of his majesty's reducing all the colonies to obedience, and he far exceeded the Assyrian general who we read of in ancient writ in blasphemy by saying that God almighty had become a Rebel, but if there were 20 Gods on that side, they would all be conquered, was his expression. Whilst he was employed in this impious blasphemy he had his officers and men taking all the horses fit for his purpose, so that many of the aged men had to walk many miles home afoot. This ill behavior of the enemy made an impression on the minds of the most serious men in this little band and raised their courage under the belief that they would be made instruments in the hand of Heaven to punish this enemy for his wickedness and blasphemy—and no doubt the recent injuries that many of their families received from the said Huck and his party had an effect to stimulate this little band to a proper courage. The number of the Americans was 133, and many of them without arms. Captain Huck had about 100 horse and Colonel Ferguson, at this time commander of the Tory militia, had about 300 men. They were encamped in a lane—a strong fence on each side—the horse picketed in the inside of a field next to the lane. . . . In the field . . . [were] a number of women, which the said Huck had brought there, and at the moment the action commenced, he was then flourishing his sword over the head of these unfortunate women, and threatening them with death if they would not get their husbands and sons to come in—and marching all night, we made the attack about the break of day. The plan was to attack both ends of the lane at the same time, but unfortunately the party sent to make the attack on the east end of the lane met with some embarrassments, by fences, brush, briars, etc., that they could not get to the end of the lane until the firing commenced at the west end. The probability is that if that party had made good their march in time very few of them [the Tories] would have escaped. However Captain Huck was killed, and also Colonel Ferguson of the Tory militia. Huck's lieutenant was wounded and died afterwards; considerable number of privates, the number not known, [were also killed], as there were many of their carcasses found in the woods some days after. This happened about the 10th of July,[2] 1780, at Williamson's Plantation in York District, and it was the first check the enemy had received after the fall of Charleston; and was of greater consequence to the American cause than can be well supposed from an affair of [so] small a magnitude—as it had the tendency to inspire the Americans with courage and fortitude and to teach them that the enemy was not invincible.

Notes

[1] William Hill, *Colonel William Hill's Memoirs of the Revolution* (Columbia: Historical Commission of South Carolina, 1921), 7–10.
[2] July 12, actually.

The Gamecock

From Colonel William Hill's Memoirs of the Revolution[1]

*After the fall of Charleston in May 1780, Thomas Sumter,
a veteran of the Cherokee wars and a colonel in the Continental
Army, accepted parole and retired to his plantation in the High
Hills of the Santee, not far from where the town bearing his name
now stands. But later that month, as Tarleton pursued Colonel
Abraham Buford's men, "Bloody Ban" sent some of his riders to
try to capture Sumter. Having been warned, Sumter escaped to
the rebel encampment in Salisbury, North Carolina, so the legion-
naires, after moving Sumter's crippled wife off the front porch,
burned his house to the ground.[2]*

*Anyone who has watched a formulaic Western or action mov-
ie has seen the moment when the villain goes too far and pushes the
hero past endurance. The hero's eyes set, the music swells, and the
audience knows that the villain's downfall has been set in motion.*

This was such a moment for the British army in the Carolinas.

When Whigs throughout the Carolinas were giving up the American cause as lost, and Cornwallis's army and loyalists were rolling unopposed through the countryside, Thomas Sumter raised a standard in North Carolina and called men to him. Before Francis Marion, before Andrew Pickens, Thomas Sumter made his stand. He set up a series of camps on the west bank of the Catawba River, each one steadily closer to, and then farther inside, the South Carolina line. Other partisan leaders such as William Bratton, Thomas Brandon, and William Hill brought their bands to Sumter's command and elected him brigadier general. Before long, Sumter's men would call him by another name: the Gamecock.

As a commander, Sumter had his faults. He was not a tactical genius like Marion, almost always preferring a frontal assault. He lacked Nathanael Greene's strategic vision. He did not have Daniel Morgan's inspiring charisma and common touch. He could be prickly and uncooperative to the point of endangering his own cause, and he never learned to sacrifice his own plans for the good of the campaign. As his nickname suggests, though, Sumter never backed down from a fight, and a fighter was what the Carolinas needed in the bleak summer of 1780. Cornwallis later described Sumter as his "greatest plague."[3]

After the war, Sumter represented South Carolina in both the United States House of Representatives and the Senate. He was 98, the oldest surviving Revolutionary War general, when he died in 1832.

William Hill left the following account of Sumter's attacks on the British posts at Rocky Mount and Hanging Rock in the South Carolina back country. Undertaken just after Huck's Defeat, Sumter's assaults—in which rebel partisans took on fortified

British positions—would have been unthinkable just a few weeks earlier. At Hanging Rock, Sumter was joined by militia from North Carolina under the redoubtable William R. Davie. Among Davie's men was the young Andrew Jackson, making this battle probably the first the future Hero of New Orleans ever saw.

Shortly after this, being the 13th July, 1780, General Sumter made an unsuccessful attempt to reduce the British post at Rocky Mount. This was made under the impression that the enemy was in a large framed house, the walls of which were of thin clapboards, and as we supposed that our balls would have the desired effect by shooting through the wall, but so it was, that from the time we received this information until the time the attack was made, the enemy had wrought day and night and had placed small logs about a foot from the inside of the wall and rammed the cavity with clay, and under this delusion we made the attack, but soon found that we could injure them no way, but by shooting in their portholes. And here the brave Colonel [Thomas] Neel was killed and seven privates; upon this we were forced to retreat behind a ledge of rocks about a hundred yards from the house. Here the officers held a council and it was discovered that there was a large rock, and between this rock and the fort, stood a small house which might be fired by throwing fire brands over the rock, and that this house would communicate the fire to the house the enemy was in and as we had the command of the water they could not possibly extinguish the flames. From this ledge of rocks where the army lay, to the rock near the house was about 100 yards, free of any obstructions; and it is well known that when any object is going from or coming to a marksman, the marksman had near as good a chance as if the object was stationary. It was then proposed by the General and other officers for two men to endeavor to fire that small house, but the undertaking appeared so hazardous, that no two men of the army could be found to undertake it. After some considerable time was spent, your author proposed that if any other man would go with him he would make the attempt; at length a young man, brother to the Johnsons now living in Fairfield District, proposed to undertake [it] with me. And we had every assistance that could be obtained—rich lightwood split and bound with cords to cover the most vital parts of our bodies, as well as a large bundle of the same wood to carry in our arms. Being thus equipped we run the 100 yards to the rock; Mr. Johnson was to manage the fire and your author was to watch the enemy's sallying out of the house. But before the fire was sufficiently kindled the enemy did sally out with fixed bayonets; the same race was run again, to where the army lay, and under a heavy fire, not only from those who had sallied out, but like wise from a large number of portholes in that end of the house. It was then proposed that the whole of our riflemen should direct their fire to that space between the small and great house, which was about 15 feet. We being equipped as before mentioned, made the second attempt, and the plan already mentioned, prevented the enemy from sallying a second time. We then had an opportunity of making a large fire behind the rock, and throwing fire brands on the roof of the little house and we stayed until that roof was in flames, and the heat of it had caused the wall of the great house to smoke. We then concluded the work was done, and undertook the fourth race, which was much more hazardous than the former ones, as the enemy during the interval, had opened a great many more portholes in that end of the building. And here I beg leave to remark that Providence so protected us both, that neither of us lost a drop of blood, although locks of hair was cut from our heads and our garments riddled with balls. And scarcely had we time to look back from behind the rock where our men lay, in hopes to see the fire progressing, but to our great mortification, when the great house was beginning to flame—as heavy a storm of rain fell, as hath fallen from that time to the present, and which extinguished the flames. We were then forced to retreat under as great mortification, as ever any number of men endured.

About the 21st of July, 1780, General Sumter made a successful attack on the British post at the Hanging Rock at which place were about 500 Regulars and about 800 Tories from North Carolina commanded by Colonel [Samuel] Bryan. General Sumter had about 600 South Carolinians. General Sumter's men were so short of ammunition, that when they began this attack generally, no one of them had more than five bullets. In the latter part of the action the arms and ammunition, which were taken from the British and Tories, who fell in the commencement of it, were turned against their associates. In this attack there was a number of men from Mecklenburg County in North Carolina commanded by Colonel Ervin [Robert Erwin], the number not known, and likewise about 80 horse commanded by Colonel Davie—these men behaved well, and are entitled to equal merit with the South Carolinians. This action commenced under many very unfavorable circumstances to the Americans, as they had to march across a water course and climb a steep cliff, being all this time under the enemy's fire and could not injure them until they got around the side of their camp. But as soon as they got to their ground they instantly drove them out of their camp and pursued them a considerable distance. In the meantime the British camp, being about one and a quarter mile from this Tory camp, advanced firing in platoons before the one half of the Americans could be brought off from the pursuit of the Tories; these few took to trees and rocks, whilst the British were advancing firing in platoons, and they fell so fast by their unseen enemy that their officers were obliged to push them forward by their sabers. The loss of the British in the action was great in killed and wounded. The Prince of Wales' regiment was almost annihilated. The Tories lost and killed was considerable. The Americans had about 40 killed, and two captains and your author wounded.

Notes

[1]William Hill, *Colonel William Hill's Memoirs of the Revolution* (Columbia: Historical Commission of South Carolina, 1921), 11–13.

[2]Walter Edgar, *Partisans and Redcoats: The Southern Conflict That Turned the Tide of the American Revolution* (New York: Harper Perennial, 2003), 61.

[3]John Buchanan, *The Road to Guilford Courthouse: The American Revolution in the Carolinas* (New York: John Wiley & Sons, 1997), 393.

A Narrative of the Battle of Camden

From "A Narrative / of the Campaign of 1780,"[1]
by Colonel Otho Holland Williams

Even before Charleston fell, George Washington sent a reinforcement of about 1,400 men south. Though few in number, and
too late to help Charleston, these men would prove invaluable over
the course of the American Revolution in the Carolinas. They were
eight regiments from the Maryland and Delaware Continental
lines, commanded by the bold and persistent General Johann de
Kalb, and they were among the best regular troops the Americans had to offer. Two of the regiments—the First Maryland and
the Delaware—had served in every major battle Washington had
fought since 1776. These veterans would provide a core to the
army in the South in every pitched battle the Continentals fought
during the following year.

After losing 5,000 men and his southern commander at

Charleston and Colonel Abraham Buford and his men at the Waxhaws, Washington wanted the Continental Congress to send his most trusted lieutenant, Nathanael Greene, to take command of what little was left of the American army in the South. Congress, though, did not ask its general's advice.[2] It chose instead General Horatio Gates, a former British army officer and "the Hero of Saratoga." Gates shared Congress's high opinion of himself, and he was not bashful about sharing that opinion with others. Though he had beaten General John "Gentleman Johnny" Burgoyne at Saratoga, a true turning point in the war, he had done so largely because Burgoyne wore his army ragged in the wilderness, and because Gates had the assistance of possibly the two finest combat commanders in the Continental Army: Daniel Morgan (see "The Battle of the Cowpens," pages 171-88) and Benedict Arnold. According to military historian W. J. Wood, Gates's indecisiveness before Saratoga drove these two warriors to distraction, but during the battle, that indecisiveness—and Gates's decision to post himself almost two miles from the battlefield—allowed them the freedom to act on their own initiative.[3]

In the Carolinas, Gates did not have a Morgan or an Arnold to fight his battles, nor was he facing another Gentleman Johnny. In the annals of the British Empire, Charles, Earl Cornwallis, may not rank in the top tier occupied by the Duke of Wellington and John Churchill, but neither does he rank much below it. Of the generals London sent to quell the American rebellion, Cornwallis was easily the most active, the most effective, and the most aggressive—ironic, considering that as a member of the House of Lords, Cornwallis had argued against the Stamp Act and had generally favored the colonies' cause.

Cornwallis remains one of the most fascinating figures of the

American Revolution. He was an aristocrat (his uncle was archbishop of Canterbury, and his great-uncle was Sir Robert Walpole), an Old Etonian, a member of George III's Privy Council despite his opposition to the king's American policies, and—by 1780—a disconsolate widower. He would go on to serve as one of the most effective and humane of Britain's governors general of India. First and last, though, Cornwallis was a professional soldier, a "man who could have thrust his hand in a flame if necessary,"[4] according to Barbara Tuchman. Commissioned an officer at age 17, he had even studied at a military school in Turin. His officers and men recognized and respected his martial spirit and his willingness to share their burdens and dangers. As a strategist, tactician, and inspirer of troops, Cornwallis had no equal in the Carolinas—yet.

Colonel Otho Holland Williams of the Maryland line left the following account of what happened when Gates stumbled into Cornwallis on the road to Camden. Williams arrived in the Carolinas as de Kalb's deputy adjutant general and would leave as one of the unsung heroes of the American Revolution. Though blunt in his description of Gates's decisions before and during the battle and the effects of those decisions, he rarely voices outright condemnation. He rarely has to.

≈

After writing [his orders for the march to Camden], the general [Gates] communicated it to the deputy adjutant general [Williams], showing him, at the same time, a rough estimate of the forces under his command, making them upwards of seven thousand. That this calculation was exaggerated, the deputy adjutant general could not but suspect, from his own observation. He, therefore, availed himself of the general's orders, to call all the general officers in the army to a council, to be held in Rugley's barn—to call also upon the commanding officers of corps for a field return; in making which, they were to be as exact as possible; and, as he was not required to attend the council, he busied himself in collecting these returns and forming an abstract for the general's better information. This abstract was presented to the general just as the council broke up, and immediately upon his coming out of the door. He cast his eyes upon the numbers of rank and file present fit for duty, which was exactly 3052. He said there were no less than 13 general officers in council; and intimated something about the disproportion between the numbers of officers and privates. It was replied, "Sir, the number of the latter are certainly much below the estimate formed this morning; but," said the general, "these are enough for our purpose." What that was, was not communicated to the deputy adjutant general. The general only added—"there was no dissenting voice in the council where the orders have just been read"—and then gave them to be published to the army.

Although there had been no dissenting voice in the council, the orders were no sooner promulgated than they became the subject of animadversion [criticism]. Even those who had been dumb in council said that there had been no consultation—that the orders were read to them, and all opinion seemed suppressed by the very positive and decisive terms in which they were expressed. Others could not imagine how it could be conceived that an army, consisting of more than two-thirds militia, and which had never been once exercised in arms together, could form columns, and perform other maneuvers in the night, and in the face of an enemy. But, of all the officers, Colonel [Charles Teffin] Armand took the greatest exception. He seemed to think the positive orders respecting himself implied a doubt of his courage—declared that cavalry had never before been put in the front of a line of battle in the dark— and that the disposition, as it respected his corps, proceeded from resentment in the general, on account of a previous altercation between them about horses, which the general had ordered to be taken from the officers of the army to expedite the movement of the artillery through the wilderness. A great deal was said upon the occasion; but, the time was short, and the officers and soldiers, generally, not knowing, or believing any more than the general, that any considerable body of the enemy were to be met with out of Camden, acquiesced with their usual cheerfulness, and were ready to march at the hour appointed.

As there were no spirits yet arrived in camp; and as, until lately, it was unusual for troops to make a forced march, or prepare to meet an enemy without some extraordinary allowance, it was unluckily conceived that molasses would, for once, be an acceptable substitute; accordingly the hospital stores were broached, and one gill of molasses per man, and a full ration of corn meal and meat, were issued to the army previous to their march, which commenced, according to orders, at about ten o'clock at night of the 15th. But I must arrest the progress of the narrative to apologize for introducing a remark, seemingly so trivial. Nothing ought to be considered as trivial, in an army, which in any degree affects the health or spirits of the troops; upon which often, more than upon numbers, the fate of battles depends. The troops of General Gates's army had frequently felt the bad consequences of eating bad provision; but, at this time, a hasty meal of quick baked bread and fresh beef, with a dessert of molasses, mixed with mush, or dumplings, operated so cathartically, as to disorder very many of the men, who were breaking the ranks all night, and were certainly much debilitated before the action commenced in the morning.

It has been observed that the direct march of the American army towards Camden, and the prospect of considerable re-enforcements of militia, had induced the [British] commanding officer, Lord Rawdon, to collect there all the forces under his directions. And it is certain that the seeming confidence of the American general had inspired him with apprehensions for his principal post. Lord Cornwallis, at Charlestown, was constantly advised of the posture of affairs in the interior of the country; and, confident that Lord Rawdon could not long resist the forces that might, and probably would, be opposed to him, in a very short time resolved to march himself, with a considerable re-enforcement, to Camden. He arrived there on the 14th, and had the discernment, at once, to perceive that delay would render that situation dangerous, even to his whole force; the disaffection of his late assumed, arbitrary, and vindictive power, having become general through all the country above General Gates's line of march, as well as to the eastward of Santee, and to the westward of Wateree rivers. He, therefore, took the resolution of attacking the new constituted American army in their open irregular encampment at Clermont. Both armies, ignorant of each other's intentions, moved about the same hour of the same night, and approaching each other, met about halfway between their respective encampments, at midnight.

The first revelation of this new and unexpected scene was occasioned by a smart mutual salutation of small arms between the advanced guards. Some of the cavalry of Armand's legion were wounded, retreated, and threw the whole corps into disorder; which, recoiling suddenly on the front of the column of infantry, disordered the first Maryland brigade, and occasioned a general consternation through the whole line of the army. The light infantry under [Lieutenant Colonel Charles] Porterfield, however, executed their orders gallantly; and the enemy, no less astonished than ourselves, seemed to acquiesce in a sudden suspension of hostilities. Some prisoners were taken on both sides; from one of these, the deputy adjutant general of the American army extorted information respecting the situation and numbers of the enemy. He informed that Lord Cornwallis commanded in person about 3000 regular British troops, which were, in line of march, about five or six hundred yards in front. Order was soon restored in the corps of infantry in the American army, and the officers were employed in forming a front line of battle, when the deputy adjutant general communicated to General Gates the information which he had from the prisoner. The general's astonishment could not be concealed. He ordered the deputy adjutant general to call another council of war. All the general officers immediately assembled in the rear of the line; the unwelcome news was communicated to them. General Gates said, "Gentlemen, what is best to be done?" All were mute for a few moments—when the gallant [brigadier general Edward] Stevens exclaimed, "Gentlemen, is it not too late *now* to do anything but fight?" No other advice was offered, and the general desired the gentlemen would repair to their respective commands.

The Baron DeKalb's opinion may be inferred from the following fact: When the deputy adjutant general went to call him to council, he first told him what had been discovered. "Well," said the baron, "and has the general given you orders to retreat the army?" The baron, however, did not oppose the suggestion of General Stevens; and every measure that ensued was preparatory for action.

Lieutenant Colonel Porterfield, in whose bravery and judicious conduct great dependence was placed, received, in the first rencontre [engagement], a mortal wound (as it long afterwards proved), and was obliged to retire. His infantry bravely kept the ground in front; and the American army were formed in the following order: The Maryland division, including the Delawares, on the right—the North Carolina militia in the center—and the Virginia militia on the left. It happened that each flank was covered by a marsh, so near as to admit the removing of the first Maryland brigade to form a second line, about 200 yards in the rear of the first. The artillery was removed from the center of the brigades and placed in the center of the front line; and the North Carolina militia (light infantry) under Major [John] Armstrong, which had retreated at the first rencontre, was ordered to cover a small interval between the left wing and the swampy grounds on that quarter.

Frequent skirmishes happened during the night between the advanced parties—which served to discover the relative situations of the two armies—and as a prelude to what was to take place in the morning.

At dawn of day (on the morning of the 16th of August) the enemy appeared in front, advancing in column. Captain [Anthony] Singleton, who commanded some pieces of artillery, observed to Colonel Williams that he plainly perceived the ground of the British uniform at about 200 yards in front. The deputy adjutant general immediately ordered Captain Singleton to open his battery; and then rode to the general, who was in the rear of the second line, and informed him of the cause of the firing which he heard. He also observed to the general that the enemy seemed to be displaying their column by the right;[5] the nature of the ground favored this conjecture, for yet nothing was clear.

The general seemed disposed to wait events—he gave no orders. The deputy adjutant general observed that if the enemy, in the act of displaying, were briskly attacked by General Stevens' brigade, which was already in line of battle, the effect might be fortunate, and first impressions were important. "Sir," said the general, "that's right—let it be done." This was the last order that the deputy adjutant general received. He hastened to General Stevens, who instantly advanced with his brigade, apparently in fine spirits. The right wing of the enemy was soon discovered in line—it was too late to attack them displaying; nevertheless, the business of the day could no longer be deferred. The deputy adjutant general requested General Stevens to let him have 40 or 50 privates, volunteers, who would run forward of the brigade and commence the attack. They were led forward, within 40 or 50 yards of the enemy, and ordered to take trees, and keep up as brisk a fire as possible. The desired effect of this expedient, to extort the enemy's fire at some distance, in order to [render] it less terrible to the militia, was not gained. General Stevens, observing the enemy to rush on, put his men in mind of their bayonets; but the impetuosity with which they advanced, firing and huzzaing, threw the whole body of the militia into such a panic that they generally threw down their loaded arms and fled in the utmost consternation. The unworthy example of the Virginians was almost instantly followed by the North Carolinians; only a small part of the brigade, commanded by Brigadier General [Isaac] Gregory, made a short pause. A part of [Lieutenant Colonel Henry] Dixon's regiment, of that brigade, next in the line to the second Maryland brigade, fired two or three rounds of cartridge. But a great majority of the militia (at least two-thirds of the army) fled without firing a shot. The writer avers it of his own knowledge, having seen and observed every part of the army, from left to right, during the action. He who has never seen the effect of panic upon a multitude can have but an imperfect idea of such a thing. The best disciplined troops have been enervated and made cowards by it. Armies have been routed by it, even where no enemy appeared to furnish an excuse. Like electricity, it operates instantaneously—like sympathy, it is irresistible where it touches. But, in the present instance, its action was not universal. The regular troops, who had the keen edge of sensibility rubbed off by strict discipline and hard service, saw the confusion with but little emotion. They engaged seriously in the affair; and, notwithstanding some irregularity, which was created by the militia breaking, pell mell, through the second line, order was restored there—time enough to give the enemy a severe check, which abated the fury of their assault, and obliged them to assume a more deliberate manner of acting. The second Maryland brigade, including the battalion of Delawares, on the right, were engaged with the enemy's left, which they opposed with very great firmness. They even advanced upon them, and had taken a number of prisoners, when their companions of the first brigade (which formed the second line) being greatly outflanked, and charged by superior numbers, were obliged to give ground. At this critical moment, the regimental officers of the latter brigade, reluctant to leave the field without orders, inquired for their commanding officer (Brigadier General Stevens), who, however, was not to be found; notwithstanding, Colonel [John] Gunby, Major Anderson, and a number of other brave officers, assisted by the deputy adjutant general, and Major Jones, one of [General William] Smallwood's aides, rallied the brigade, and renewed the contest. Again they were obliged to give way—and were again rallied—the second brigade were still warmly engaged—the distance between the two brigades did not exceed 200 yards—their opposite flanks being nearly upon a line perpendicular to their front. At this eventful juncture, the deputy adjutant general, anxious that the communication between them should be preserved, and wishing that, in the almost certain event of a retreat, some order might be sustained by them, hastened from the first to the second brigade, which he found precisely in the same circumstances. He called upon his own regiment (the 6th Maryland) not to fly, and was answered by the Lieutenant Colonel, [Benjamin] Ford, who said—"They have done all that can be expected of them— we are outnumbered and outflanked—see the enemy charge with bayonets." The enemy having collected their corps, and directing their whole force against these two devoted brigades, a tremendous fire of musketry was, for some time, kept up on both sides, with equal perseverance and obstinacy, until Lord Cornwallis, perceiving there was no cavalry opposed to him, pushed forward his dragoons—and his infantry charging, at the same moment, with fixed bayonets, put an end to the contest. His victory was complete. All the artillery, and a very great number of prisoners, fell into his hands—many fine fellows lay on the field—and the rout of the remainder was entire—not even a company retired in any order—every one escaped as he could. If, in this affair, the militia fled too soon, the regulars may be thought almost as blamable for remaining too long on the field; especially, after all hope of victory must have been despaired of. Let the commandants of the brigades answer for themselves. Allow the same privilege to the officers of the corps, comprising those brigades, and they will say that they never received orders to retreat, nor any order from any general officer, from the commencement of the action until it became desperate. The brave Major General, the Baron DeKalb, fought on foot, with the second brigade, and fell, mortally wounded, into the hands of the enemy, who stripped him even of his shirt; a fate which probably was avoided by other generals only by an opportune retreat.

The torrent of unarmed militia bore away with it Generals Gates, [Richard] Caswell, and a number of others, who soon saw that all was lost. General Gates, at first, conceived a hope that he might rally, at Clermont, a sufficient number to cover the retreat of the regulars; but the farther they fled the more they were dispersed; and the generals soon found themselves abandoned by all but their aides. Lieutenant Colonel [John Christian] Senf, who had been on the expedition with Colonel [Thomas] Sumter, returned, and overtaking General Gates, informed him of their complete success—that the enemy's redoubt, on Wateree, opposite to Camden, was first reduced, and the convoy of stores, etc., from Charleston was decoyed, and became prize to the American party, almost without resistance. That upwards of 100 prisoners, and 40 loaded wagons, were in the hands of the party, who had sustained very little loss; but the general could avail himself nothing of this trifling advantage. The detachment under Sumter was on the opposite side of the Wateree, marching off, as speedily as might be, to secure their booty—for the course of the firing in the morning indicated unfavorable news from the army.

The militia, the general saw, were in air; and the regulars, he feared, were no more. The dreadful thunder of artillery and musketry had ceased, and none of his friends appeared. There was not existing corps with which the victorious detachment might unite; and the Americans had no post in the rear. He, therefore, sent orders to Sumter to retire in the best manner he could; and proceeded himself with General Caswell towards Charlotte, an open village on a plain, about 60 miles from the fatal scene of action. The Virginians, who knew nothing of the country they were in, involuntarily reversed the route they came, and fled, most of them, to Hillsborough. General Stevens pursued them, and halted there as many as were not sufficiently refreshed before his arrival to pursue their way home. Their terms of service, however, being very short, and no prospect presenting itself to afford another proof of their courage, General Stevens soon afterwards discharged them.

The North Carolina militia fled different ways, as their hopes led, or their fears drove them. Most of them[,] preferring the shortest way home, scattered through the wilderness which lies between Wateree and Pee Dee Rivers, and thence towards Roanoke. Whatever these might have suffered from the disaffected, they probably were not worse off than those who retired the way they came; wherein, they met many of their insidious friends, armed, and advancing to join the American army; but, learning its fate from the refugees, they acted decidedly in concert with the victors; and, captivating some, plundering others, and maltreating all the fugitives they met, returned, exultingly, home. They even added taunts to their perfidy; one of a party, who robbed Brigadier General [John] Butler of his sword, consoled him by saying, "You'll have no further use for it."

The regular troops, it has been observed, were the last to quit the field. Every corps was broken and dispersed; even the bogs and brush, which in some measure served to screen them from their furious pursuers, separated them from one another. Major Anderson was the only officer who fortunately rallied, as he retreated, a few men of different companies; and whose prudence and firmness afforded protection to those who joined his party on the route.

Colonel Gunby, Lieutenant Colonel [John Eager] Howard, Captain [Robert] Kirkwood, and Captain [Henry] Dobson, with a few other officers, and 50 or 60 men, formed a junction on the route, and proceeded together.

The general order for moving off the heavy baggage, etc., to Waxhaws, was not put in execution, as directed to be done, on the preceding evening. The whole of it, consequently, fell into the hands of the enemy; as well as all that which followed the army except the wagons of the Generals Gates and DeKalb; which, being furnished with the stoutest horses, fortunately escaped, under the protection of a small quarter guard. Other wagons also had got out of danger from the enemy; but the cries of the women and the wounded in the rear, and the consternation of the flying troops, so alarmed some of the wagoners that they cut out their teams, and taking each a horse, left the rest for the next that should come. Others were obliged to give up their horses to assist in carrying off the wounded; and the whole road, for many miles, was strewed with signals of distress, confusion, and dismay. What added not a little to this calamitous scene was the conduct of Armand's legion. They were principally foreigners, and some of them, probably, not unaccustomed to such scenes. Whether it was owing to the disgust of the colonel at general orders, or the cowardice of his men, is not with the writer to determine; but, certain it is, the legion did not take any part in the action of the 16th; they retired early, and in disorder, and were seen plundering the baggage of the army on their retreat. One of them cut Captain [William] Lemar, of the Maryland infantry, over the hand, for attempting to reclaim his own portmanteau, which the fellow was taking out of the wagon. Captain Lemar was unarmed, having broke his sword in action, and was obliged to submit both to the loss and to the insult. The tent covers were thrown off the wagons, generally, and the baggage exposed, so that one might take what suited him to carry off. General Caswell's mess wagons afforded the best refreshment; very unexpectedly to the writer, he there found a pipe of good Madeira, broached, and surrounded by a number of soldiers, whose appearance led him to inquire what engaged their attention. He acknowledges that in this instance he shared in the booty, and took a draught of wine, which was the only refreshment he had received that day.

But the catastrophe being over, before we pursue a detail of all its distressing consequences, it may be excusable to consider whether the measures which led to the necessity of fighting a general battle were justifiable: and whether such an event might not have been avoided at almost any time before the two armies were actually opposed?

If General Gates *intended* to risk a general action, conscious of all circumstances, he certainly made that risk under every possible disadvantage; and a contemplation of those circumstances would seem to justify Colonel Armand's assertion, made in the afternoon of the day in which the battle was fought—"I will not," said he, "say that we have been betrayed, but if it had been the purpose of the general to sacrifice his army, what could he have done more effectually to have answered that purpose?"

NOTES

[1]William Johnson, *Sketches of the Life and Correspondence of Nathanael Greene, Major General of the Armies of the United States, in the War of the Revolution*, vol. 1 (Charleston. S.C.: A. E. Miller, 1822), 493–99.

[2]John S. Pancake, *This Destructive War: The British Campaign in the Carolinas, 1780–1782* (Tuscaloosa: University of Alabama Press, 1985), 99.

[3]W. J. Wood, *Battles of the Revolutionary War, 1775–1781* (Chapel Hill, N.C.: Algonquin Books of Chapel Hill, 1990), 150–71.

[4]Barbara Tuchman, *The First Salute: A View of the American Revolution* (New York: Ballantine Books, 1989), 285.

[5]"Displaying" means moving from march formation to battle formation; it presents an opportune time for an enemy to attack.

PART III

The Partisans Rise
September – October 1780

The Swamp Fox

From *The Life of General Francis Marion*,[1]
by Brigadier General Peter Horry and Parson M. L. Weems

As the British army approached Charleston, a group of Continental officers stationed in the city gathered for dinner and, afterwards, a drinking game. One officer—a small, quiet South Carolinian—attempted to decline, but his fellows barred the door of their upstairs room and insisted he join them. The quiet officer was equally insistent that he would not. He went to the window and jumped to the street below, breaking his ankle. Unfit for duty, he was sent home to recuperate.[2]

So when the Charleston garrison surrendered, Francis Marion was not there. Over the coming year, Marion would make a habit of not being where he was expected to be.

At first glance, Marion would seem an unlikely partisan leader, much less the most celebrated partisan leader the American

Revolution produced. He was small, in a time and place that expected its warrior chiefs to be physically imposing men like Daniel Morgan and George Washington. He was quiet and reserved, especially when compared to leaders like Thomas Sumter. As he showed by jumping out that window, though, Marion was also stubborn, creative, and bold. He would prove himself to be a brilliant tactician, one who could learn from his mistakes, recognize and exploit opportunities, and—most importantly—reliably win his fights.

Marion was born in 1732. He served under William Moultrie in South Carolina's war on the Cherokees in the 1760s, once leading an advance party of 30 men into a mountain pass where Marion knew they would be ambushed. Marion fought off the Cherokees at the cost of all but eight of his men.[3] The coming of the American Revolution brought him out of a peaceful life of hunting and fishing on his Santee River plantation. He again served under Moultrie at the first, successful defense of Sullivan's Island.

Unlike most partisans, Marion was an officer of the Continental Army. When Horatio Gates arrived in the Carolinas, Marion reported to the commanding general, awaiting orders. Gates, unimpressed by Marion and his small, filthy, motley force, sent them off to scout the interior while he continued his march to Camden.[4] Marion thus escaped a second American disaster at which his military genius would have made no difference. He went on to wage the small-scale, irregular warfare that made him "the Swamp Fox."

Though known to be a strict disciplinarian, he was not troubled by the unreliable nature of militia. He preferred to work with a small force, as was best suited to his guerrilla strategies, so he let men serve with him as long as they felt like it. His band was some-

times as large as several hundred, sometimes as small as 20.[5]

The following account was written by Peter Horry, one of the few men Marion allowed into his confidence.[6] The account was embellished, though, by Parson Mason Locke Weems, who made a nice living by retelling the exploits of Revolutionary War heroes, and a nicer living by making them up when he had to (among his inventions was the story of George Washington chopping down the cherry tree). Though Horry was appalled by Weems's decorations, the incidents remain essentially as Horry described them. This excerpt tells of Marion's reaction to the American defeat at Camden and captures the essence of his effectiveness; even in the aftermath of as complete a victory as Camden, the British found they could not be safe in "conquered" Carolina.

~

The history of the American Revolution is a history of miracles. . . .

Some of our chimney-corner philosophers can hardly believe, when they read of Samson making such a smash among the Philistines with the jawbone of an ass. Then how will they believe what I am going to tell them of Marion? How will they believe that, at a time when the British had completely overrun South Carolina; their headquarters at Charleston, a victorious army at Camden; strong garrisons at Georgetown and Jacksonborough, with swarms of thievish and bloody-minded Tories, filling up all between; and the spirits of the poor Whigs so completely cowed, that they were fairly knocked under to the civil and military yoke of the British, who, I ask again, will believe, that in this desperate state of things, one little, swarthy, French-phizzed Carolinian, with only 30 of his ragged countrymen, issuing out of the swamps, should have dared to turn his horse's head towards this all-conquering foe?

Well, Marion was that man. He it was, who, with his feeble force, dared to dash up at once to Nelson's ferry, on the great war path between the British armies at Charleston and Camden.

"Now, my gallant friends," said he, at sight of the road, and with a face burning for battle, "now look sharp! Here are the British wagon tracks, with the sand still falling in! And here are the steps of their troops passing and repassing. We shall not long be idle here!"

And so it turned out. For scarcely had we reached our hiding place in the swamp, before in came our scouts at half speed, stating that a British guard, with a world of American prisoners, were on their march for Charleston.

"How many prisoners do you suppose there were?" said Marion.

"Near two hundred," replied the scouts.

"And what do you imagine was the number of the British guard?"

"Why, sir, we counted about ninety."

"Ninety!" said Marion with a smile, "Ninety! Well, that will do. And now, gentlemen, if you will only stand by me, I've a good hope that we thirty will have those ninety by tomorrow's sunrise."

We told him to lead on, for that we were resolved to die by his side.

Soon as the dusky night came on, we went down to the ferry, and passing for a party of good loyalists, we easily got set over. The enemy, with their prisoners, having just effected the passage of the river as the sun went down, halted at the first tavern, generally called "the Blue House," where the officers ordered supper. In front of the building was a large arbor, wherein the topers [drunkards] were wont to sit, and spend the jocund night away in songs and gleeful draughts of apple brandy grog. In this arbor, flushed with their late success, sat the British guard; and tickler [drink] after tickler swilling, roared it away to the tune of "Britannia Strike Home": till overcome with fatigue, and the opiate juice, down they sunk, deliciously beastified, to the ground.

Just as the cock had winded his last horn for day we approached the house in perfect concealment, behind a string of fence, within a few yards of it. But in spite of all our address, we could not effect a complete surprisal of them. Their sentinels took the alarm, and firing their pieces, fled into the yard. Swift as lightning we entered with them, and seizing their muskets, which were all stacked near the gate, we made prisoners of the whole party, without having been obliged to kill more than three of them.

Had Washington and his whole army been upon the survivors, they could hardly have roared out louder for quarter. After securing their arms, Marion called for their captain; but he was not to be found, high nor low, among the living or dead. However, after a hot search, he was found up the chimney! He begged very hard that we would not let his men know where he had concealed himself. Nothing could equal the mortification of the British, when they came to see what a handful of militia-men had taken them, and recovered all their prisoners.

Marion was at first in high hopes that the American regulars whom he had so gallantly rescued would, to a man, have joined his arms, and fought hard to avenge their late defeat. But equally to his surprise and their own disgrace, not one of them could be prevailed on to shoulder a musket! "Where is the use," said they, "of fighting now, when all is lost?"

This was the general impression. And indeed except these unconquerable spirits, Marion and Sumter, with a few others of the same heroic stamp, who kept the field, Carolina was no better than a British province.

In our late attack on the enemy, we had but four rounds of powder and ball, and not a single sword that deserved the name. But Marion soon remedied that defect. He bought up all the old saw blades from the mills, and gave them to the smiths, who presently manufactured for us a parcel of substantial broadswords, sufficient, as I have often seen, to kill a man at a single blow.

From our prisoners in the late action, we got completely armed; a couple of English muskets, with bayonets and cartouche-boxes [cartridge boxes], to each of us, with which we retreated into Britton's Neck.

We had not been there above twenty-four hours before news was brought us by a trusty friend that the Tories, on Pee Dee, were mustering in force, under a Captain [Jesse] Barfield. This, as we learnt afterwards, was one of the companies that my uncle's old coachman had been so troubled about. We were quickly on horseback, and after a brisk ride of forty miles, came upon their encampment, at three o'clock in the morning. Their surprise was so complete that they did not fire a single shot! Of 49 men, who composed their company, we killed and took about 30. The arms, ammunition, and horses of the whole party, fell into our hands, with which we returned to Britton's Neck, without the loss of a man.

The rumor of these two exploits soon reached the British and their friends the Tories, who presently dispatched three stout companies to attack us. Two of the parties were British; one of them commanded by Major [James] Wemyss, of house-burning memory. The third party were altogether Tories. We fled before them towards North Carolina. Supposing they had entirely scouted us, they gave over the chase, and retreated for their respective stations; the British to Georgetown, and the Tories to Black Mingo. Learning this, from the swift mounted scouts whom he always kept close hanging upon their march, Marion ordered us to face about, and dog them to their encampment, which we attacked with great fury. Our fire commenced on them at but a short distance, and with great effect; but outnumbering us, at least two to one, they stood their ground and fought desperately. But losing their commander, and being hard pressed, they at length gave way, and fled in the utmost precipitation, leaving upwards of two-thirds of their number killed and wounded on the ground. The surprise and destruction of the Tories would have been complete, had it not been for the alarm given by our horses' feet in passing Black Mingo bridge, near which they were encamped. Marion never afterwards suffered us to cross a bridge in the night, until we had first spread our blankets on it, to prevent noise.

This third exploit of Marion rendered his name very dear to the poor Whigs, but utterly abominable to the enemy, particularly the Tories, who were so terrified at this last handling that, on their retreat, they would not halt a moment at Georgetown, though 20 miles from the field of battle, but continued their flight, not thinking themselves safe, until they had got Santee River between him and them.

NOTES

[1] Peter Horry and M. L. Weems, *The Life of General Francis Marion* (Winston-Salem, N.C.: John F. Blair, Publisher, 2000), 105–9.

[2] Ibid., 64.

[3] John Buchanan, *The Road to Guilford Courthouse: The American Revolution in the Carolinas* (New York: John Wiley & Sons, 1997), 151.

[4] Ibid., 153.

[5] John S. Pancake, *This Destructive War: The British Campaign in the Carolinas, 1780–1782* (Tuscaloosa: University of Alabama Press, 1985), 111.

[6] Ibid.

The Hornet's Nest

From *The Revolutionary War Sketches of William R. Davie*[1] and from *A History of the Campaigns of 1780 and 1781 in the Southern Provinces of North America*, by Banastre Tarleton[2]

With Horatio Gates and the Continental Army out of the way, Lord Cornwallis continued his plan to pacify South Carolina, but Thomas Sumter, Francis Marion, and the other partisans refused to be pacified. They not only kept the British army in a near-constant state of alert, they also prevented the outpouring of loyalist sympathy that the British still thought to be imminent.

Though Sir Henry Clinton had ordered him to secure only South Carolina, Cornwallis decided this could not be done without first securing North Carolina, which he assumed (correctly, to an extent) to be the partisans' source of supplies and support. As the summer of 1780 came to an end, Cornwallis moved his army north, first into the Waxhaws and then on to Charlotte.

The land that would become Charlotte was settled in 1755, when Thomas Spratt and Thomas Polk decided on a hilltop where two Native American trading paths crossed. This prime location fueled the town's rapid growth, and in 1762 a new county was carved out of the western portion of Anson County. It was named Mecklenburg in honor of the birthplace of George III's new queen, Charlotte, whose given name was adopted by the town when it was incorporated six years later. When a city grid was laid out in 1770, the trading route running north-south was named Tryon Street, for the royal governor, while the east-west path was named Trade Street.

Ironic, then, that a population that had so blatantly courted the favor of the royal government would prompt Cornwallis, when he left in October, to call Charlotte "a damn'd hornet's nest of rebellion."

In 1775, Mecklenburg's citizens had already become (maybe) the first Americans to call for independence from Great Britain (see "The Meck Dec," pages 3-15). In 1780, they made the lives of Cornwallis and his troops a living hell. What remained of the Continental Army in the Carolinas, along with the bulk of the mustered militia, had retreated to Salisbury when word came of Cornwallis's approach. William R. Davie, now a colonel, and his mounted partisans received orders to observe and, if possible with safety, harass the British as they approached. Davie posted his men behind houses, fences, and the wall of the Mecklenburg County Courthouse at the intersection of Trade and Tryon. Among the forces opposing them was Tarleton's feared British Legion—except Tarleton, sick with fever, was not there. The legion was under the command of Major George Hanger, a fine officer but also one who lacked Tarleton's boldness.

The first account, Davie's, describes his defense of Charlotte and his guerrilla strategy once the British were in the town. The second, Tarleton's, confirms that Davie's efforts were as effective as he hoped.

≈

From *The Revolutionary War Sketches* of William R. Davie

As the Waxhaws had been taxed with the supplies and even depredations of both parties it was impossible for the British army to continue their position there, and his Lordship's [Cornwallis's] plan of operations was to carry the war into North Carolina. On the 24th of September our patrols gave information that the enemy were in motion on the Steele Creek road leading to Charlotte. General [Jethro] Sumner and [William Lee] Davidson immediately retreated by the nearest route to Phifers road towards Salisbury, leaving Charlotte considerably to the left; Colonel Davie with 150 men consisting of mounted infantry and dragoons, with some volunteers under the command of a Major [Joseph] Graham, was ordered to attend the enemy's motions and skirmish with their front; this party hovered around the British army and on the evening and night of the 25th captured a number of prisoners, and about midnight took post at Charlotte, seven miles from the place where Cornwallis encamped. Early in the morning of the 26th the Colonel's patrols were driven in by the enemy's light troops, and in a few minutes the Legion and light infantry were seen advancing towards the town, followed by the whole army. The town, situated on rising ground, contains about 20 houses built on two streets, which cross each other at right angles in the intersection of which stands the courthouse. The left of the town as the enemy came up was an open common, the right was covered with under wood up to the gardens. The colonel was enforced in the night by Major Graham with 14 volunteers, and relying on the firmness of the militia, was determined to give his Lordship some earnest of what he might expect in North Carolina. For this purpose he dismounted one company and posted them under the courthouse where they were covered breast-high by a stone wall; the two other companies were advanced about 80 yards and posted behind some houses and gardens on each side of the street. While this disposition was making[,] the Legion was forming at the distance of [300 yards] with a front to fill the street, and the light infantry on their flank; on sounding the charge the cavalry advanced in full gallop within 60 yards of the courthouse when the Americans received orders to fire. This fell with such effect among the cavalry that they retreated with great precipitation, as the light infantry behaved with more resolution, and were pressing forward on our right flank notwithstanding a warm fire from the volunteers, who were too few to keep them in check. It became necessary to withdraw the two advanced companies and they were formed in a line with those at the courthouse. The flanks were hotly engaged with the infantry but the center was directed to reserve their fire for the cavalry, who rallied on their former ground, and returned to the charge. They were again well received by the militia and galloped off in the outmost confusion, in the presence of the whole British army. The Legion infantry were now beginning to turn the Colonel's right flank, and the companies were drawn off in good order, successively covering each other, and formed in a single line at the end of the street about 100 yards from the courthouse, under a galling fire from the British light infantry, who advanced under the cover of the houses and gardens. The British cavalry soon appeared again, charging in columns by the courthouse, but on receiving a fire reserved for them by a part of the militia, they wheeled off behind the houses, Lord Cornwallis vexed at the repeated repulses of his cavalry. The Legion infantry thus reinforced pressed forward rapidly on their flanks. The ground was no longer tenable by the handful of brave men, and a retreat was ordered by the Salisbury road; the enemy followed with great caution and respect for some miles, when they at length ventured to charge the rear guard. The guard were of course put to flight, but on receiving a fire from a single company the cavalry again retreated. The loss of the Americans consisted of Lieutenant [George] Locke and four privates killed, Major Graham and five privates wounded. The British stated their loss at 12 noncommissioned officers killed and wounded; Major [George] Hanger, Captains [Charles] Campbell and [Charles] McDonald wounded with about 30 privates.

This action, although it carries a charge of temerity on the part of Colonel Davie and can only be excused by the event and that zeal which we are always ready to applaud, furnishes a very striking instance of the bravery and importance of the American militia; few examples can be shewn of any troops who in one action changed their position twice in good order although pressed by a much superior body of infantry and charged three times by thrice their number of cavalry, unsupported and in the presence of the enemy's whole army and finally retreating in perfect order.

The British, chagrined to see their laurels snatched from their army by this detachment of militia, loudly charged the Legion with pusillanimity, while they excused themselves by saying that the confidence with which the Americans acted induced them to apprehend an ambuscade; surely no maneuver of this kind could be seriously expected in an open village in open day. . . .

Colonel Davie joined the army in Salisbury next day when the officers who had received commissions to recruit had assembled with the men they had raised, and Colonel [Thomas] Taylor's regiment from Granville also passed under his command so that his corps now consisted of near 300 mounted infantry with a few dragoons. Generals Sumner and Davidson continued their retreat beyond the Yadkin and Colonel Davie returned towards Charlotte. As his [Davie's] force was insufficient to make any impression on the enemy in their camp, all that could be done was to confine them if possible to the town by attacking their foraging parties, and to distress them by cutting off their supplies; in consequence of which, positions were chosen within 15 and 20 miles, and parties detached on all sides to watch and harass the enemy; he was confined by express orders to remain always with the princip[al] body in the directions between Salisbury and Charlotte, and by no means to risk being generally engaged. These orders limited the operations of this partisan but much was done by his perfect knowledge of the country and the daring bravery of the militia under his command: no party of the enemy ventured out without being attacked, and often retired with considerable loss; the people of the neighboring country were strongly

attached to the American cause, and gave his Lordship no assistance, and all information was cut off by the vigilance and
activity of the militia cavalry. However strange it may appear,
his Lordship began to feel the greatest distress, under this species of blockade, for provisions, forage, and all the necessary
supplies of an army[,] and these circumstances combined with
[Patrick] Ferguson's defeat [at Kings Mountain] determined
him to relinquish the conquest of North Carolina for the campaign, and accordingly on the night of the 14th of October he
began his retreat to South Carolina. The night was cloudy, his
Lordship was deserted by his guides, and soon fell into difficulties; so much had the Americans gained the ascendancy
that from the fire of a small party of the militia on patrol they
left 20 wagons containing a large part of the baggage of the
71st Regiment and Legion infantry.

Lord Cornwallis had intended to cross the Catawba river,
at the old Nation ford, but a sudden swell of the river obliged
him to halt the army. After remaining here two days in a miser-
able situation without supplies, surrounded by militia cavalry
who prevented all foraging, they marched precipitately down
the [east side of the] river attended by the detachment of cavalry under Colonel Davie, who continued skirmishing with
their rear [during the entire march]. On the 19th they evacuated the state and crossed the Catawba river at Lands-Ford.

From *A History of the Campaigns of 1780 and 1781 in the Southern Provinces of North America*, by Banastre Tarleton

Charlotte town afforded some conveniencies, blended with great disadvantages. The mills in its neighborhood were supposed of sufficient consequence to render it for the present an eligible position, and, in future, a necessary post, when the army advanced. But the aptness of its intermediate situation between Camden and Salisbury, and the quantity of its mills, did not counterbalance its defects. The town and environs abounded with inveterate enemies; the plantations in the neighborhood were small and uncultivated; the roads narrow, and crossed in every direction; and the whole face of the country covered with close and thick woods. In addition to these disadvantages, no estimation could be made of the sentiments of half the inhabitants of North Carolina, whilst the royal army remained at Charlotte town. It was evident, and it had been frequently mentioned to the King's officers, that the counties of Mecklenburg and Rohan [Rowan] were more hostile to England than any others in America. The vigilance and animosity of these surrounding districts checked the exertions of the well affected, and totally destroyed all communication between the King's troops and the loyalists in the other parts of the province. No British commander could obtain any information in that position, which would facilitate his designs, or guide his future conduct. Every report concerning the measures of the governor and assembly would undoubtedly be ambiguous; accounts of the preparations of the militia could only be vague and uncertain; and all intelligence of the real force and movements of the continentals must be totally unattainable.

The foraging parties were every day harassed by the inhabitants, who did not remain at home to receive payment for the produce of their plantations, but generally fired from covert places, to annoy the British detachments. Ineffectual attempts were made upon convoys coming from Camden, and the intermediate post at Blair's mill; but individuals with expresses [dispatches] were frequently murdered. An attack was directed against the picket at Polk's mill, two miles from the town: The Americans were gallantly received by Lieutenant [Stephen] Guyon, of the 23rd regiment, and the fire of his party from a loop-holed building adjoining the mill repulsed the assailants. Notwithstanding the different checks and losses sustained by the militia of the district, they continued their hostilities with unwearied perseverance; and the British troops were so effectually blockaded in their present position that very few, out of a great number of messengers, could reach Charlotte town in the beginning of October, to give intelligence of Ferguson's situation [see "Kings Mountain," pages 151-70].

Notes

[1]Blackwell P. Robinson, ed., *The Revolutionary War Sketches of William R. Davie* (Raleigh: North Carolina Department of Cultural Resources, Division of Archives and History, 1976), 21–25.

[2]Banastre Tarleton, *A History of the Campaigns of 1780 and 1781 in the Southern Provinces of North America* (Dublin: printed for Colles, Exshaw, White, H. Whitestone, Burton, etc., 1787), 159–61.

Aunt Susie and Andy Jackson

By Dr. John H. Gibbon, in a letter to the
National Intelligencer, August 29, 1845[1]

*As the British moved north from Camden through the Wax-
haws and on to Charlotte, they pushed a stream of refugees ahead
of them. The residents of the Waxhaws, having seen the aftermath
of Colonel Abraham Buford's stand against Tarleton (see "Buford's
Quarter," pages 65-72), knew well what the British could do, and
had no desire to find out what the British would do. Among the
refugees were a widow named Elizabeth Jackson and two of her
sons, Robert and Andrew; her oldest son, Hugh, had already died
in the war. Robert and Andrew had both served with William R.
Davie at Hanging Rock and other skirmishes, but facing Cornwallis was another matter. Elizabeth and her boys sought shelter*

near Charlotte until Cornwallis withdrew to his winter camp in Winnsboro, South Carolina.

Though Cornwallis had departed, the Tories had not, and the war was far from over for the Jacksons. Some of the most savage partisan fighting of the entire war raged through the Waxhaws in 1781. Robert and Andrew both took part—not this time as scouts or messengers, but as armed combatants. When the British sent a troop of dragoons to assist the Waxhaws Tories, Andrew was one of about 40 rebels who rode out to meet them. The dragoons easily scattered their opposition, and Andrew spent the next 36 hours in hiding. Faint with hunger, he made his way to his aunt's house in hopes of some food, but Tory spies spotted him and called the dragoons. The British ransacked the house, while their commanding officer unwittingly entered American legend by ordering Andrew to clean his boots.

Anyone familiar with the story of Old Hickory knows the rest: Andrew Jackson refused, claiming the status of a prisoner of war; the officer swung his saber at Jackson's head, but Jackson raised his left arm in time to ward off the brunt of the blow. Jackson carried the scars on his face and arm for the rest of his life. He and his brother were marched 40 miles to the British prison camp at Camden, where they were held until their mother negotiated their release. They then walked the 40 miles home. Both boys had contracted smallpox in the camp; Robert died, while Andrew recovered. Once Andrew's recovery was complete, his mother left for Charleston to care for her nephews, who were also British prisoners. There, she contracted cholera and died.[2]

The American Revolution in the Carolinas turned Andrew Jackson into a veteran soldier, an orphan, and an inveterate hater of the English. This hatred would have an impact on American *history far beyond the Revolutionary War and the Waxhaws. Several Jackson biographers, including H. W. Brands and John Buchanan, argue that Jackson's Anglophobia was a primary factor in his aggressive expansionism, including his removal of the Cherokees and other Native American tribes from their lands east of the Mississippi, as he sought to defend American borders from British influence and invasion.*[3]

None of that could have been guessed in September 1780, when Andy Jackson was just a boy on what must have seemed like an adventure.

The following account was taken down in 1845 by Dr. John H. Gibbon, the superintendent of the United States Mint at Charlotte and a practicing physician. He claimed to have met a Mrs. Susan Smart Alexander, also known as "Aunt Susie," during his rounds. She told him the following story about the American Revolution in the Carolinas and the future president.

Aunt Susie's story was immediately and almost entirely discredited, as the dates and facts did not mesh with the known record; she claimed, for instance, that Robert Jackson was already dead in September 1780. The account's primary usefulness is as a record of what passed for ordinary life—chores, child rearing, and charity—in an extraordinary time.

~

"Andy Jackson!" cried the old lady. "Oh! I mind [remember] Andy Jackson well; and I have no doubt he would mind me, too.

"He and his mother—Aunt Betty, we called her (her name was Elizabeth)—her sister and brother-in-law (John McKamie), and a black girl, named Charlotte, with several horses, fled before the British, from the Waxhaws, and came to reside at my father's house. They told us they just come in to stay under our roof, and we just told them to stay. My husband was in arms, and we all four gathered at my father's for convenience. Andy Jackson and his mother came up from Waxhaws about six weeks before the British came to Charlotte. The old woman lamented very much, every now and then, about things being left in such desolation at home. She acknowledged she did think of the leeks and onions of Egypt [a biblical reference from Numbers 11:5].

"She was a fresh-looking, fair-haired, very conversive, old Irish lady, at dreadful enmity with the Indians. I thought her eldest son was killed by them.[4] They did lament about their eldest son and brother. They took great spells of mourning about him. Andy was her youngest child. He was a tall young fellow, about 11 or 12 years of age. He was a lank, leaning-forward fellow, tall of his age, and a poor, grip[p]y-looking fellow, but with a large forehead and big eyes. He never was pretty, but there was something very agreeable about him. I thought him a mighty good boy—very cheerful, observing and trying to improve.

"Andy was dressed in homespun, like we all were. They did go in coarse fare during the Revolution; but, indeed, one man then was worth two men now, generally speaking.

"They were healthful, unlearned men; but there are some much more ignorant now.

". . . Andy was an independent boy in his manner and had good sense. I considered he would make a fine man then.

"But dear me! I have heard stories enough of Andy Jackson

to fill a book, but I never liked to believe them, for he was a good boy, and very fond of his mother.

"His mother could not be idle. She could spin flax beautiful. We had not cotton then. She was the busiest that could be, as if she was working for wages; but there was no price or charge, either upon work or victuals, in those days.

"Every one did whatever they could turn their hand to. She spun us heddle-yarn for weaving cloth and the best and finest I ever saw.

"They were very anxious about home—I mean she was. He never fretted—was quite happy, like [any other] boy. His mother moaned about home, as any other old body would; but, whiles, she would be very cheerful.

"It was a time of great trials.

"She did think a dreadful deal of that son, Andy, who was her all.

"Andy and I tended the farm. His mother allowed him to work at every thing he would, and he was very willing.

"We had a large new field, just cleared, planted in corn and pumpkins. Andy and I had the greatest time to keep up the fences to keep the hogs out.

"For the horsemen—the flying infantry, as they were called—were always riding about, and would throw down the fences, without ever stopping to put them up again.

"They would never go round a rod—being always in a hurry.

"Andy would cut up pumpkins and feed that cow; and he liked to look at her eating. We fed her beautifully and she gave plenty of milk.

"The Jacksons had rode upon horses, that were kept in a

back pasture well out of sight.

"Andy made bows and arrows, and shot birds about. There were many birds about in those days—snipes, partridges and wild turkeys. He had a great idea of some military business.

"I like to see a big forehead and large eyes when I want to see a martial man.

"Andy could not well be idle. He used to carry my baby about and nurse it bravely. He was very willing to do so.

"It was in a peach and watermelon time they were here. We got a good deal of support out of the corn field. We were well off. . . . Our wants were not so many, and were the easiest supplied.

"We had Continental and Convention money plenty, but it was very light [worth very little]. Some of the big folks issued their own paper for small sums, for change, payable in one year; but a great deal of it never came back to be paid. People were not anxious about money. Money was a small matter in those days. Nothing attracted their attention but liberty. That was their whole object.

"My biggest brothers had gone to the war. My husband was in the army, and I had my first baby in my arms. My mother was heavy-footed at the time—far gone with her last infant, but she could take care of my child.

"Andy and I spread flax, watered and gathered it. We had no cotton at all. He and I packed away the flax in the loft.

"The people hided all their boys, for fear the British would take them off. The men were all gone away to the army, and even the women into remote settlements, to be out of the way of the British—such a character had come from the lower country of their acts.

"I had no idea of going away. I never was afraid, thank God! My mother was too heavy-footed to go, and I had to stay with her.

"But the British were often sore belied in my notion. It was the Tories did the most mischief.

"The Hessians were exactly heathens! The British told them they must fight to the death, for, if the Americans took them prisoner they would eat them.

"But it must be said to the credit of the Americans, they never abused a prisoner yet—unless it was now and then to tar and feather a Tory. This neither broke their bones nor scalded their heads, but kept them busy getting it off them, and I thought no harm of that at all.

"The Jacksons got round and went home behind the British, as they came to Charlotte."

Notes

[1]William A. Graham, *General Joseph Graham and His Papers on North Carolina Revolutionary History* (Raleigh, N.C.: Edwards & Broughton, 1904), 71–74.

[2]H. W. Brands, *Andrew Jackson: His Life and Times* (New York: Doubleday, 2005), 26–28.

[3]John Buchanan, *Jackson's Way: Andrew Jackson and the People of the Western Waters* (New York: John Wiley & Sons, 2001), 302.

[4]Hugh Jackson was in fact killed by the British while fighting as part of a rebel militia.

Fanning's
"Rules and Regulations"

From *The Narrative of Colonel David Fanning*[1]

Most combatants in the Revolutionary War in the Carolinas
were partisans or militia. Their organization was, by definition,
fluid and adaptable, a fact that drove officers of the regular armies
to distraction (see "The Battle of the Cowpens," pages 171-88).
The extent of the organization—or lack thereof—of these fighters varied greatly from one partisan band to another. Some bands
were little more than armed gangs, with virtually no military discipline; others, such as William R. Davie's and Francis Marion's,
allowed men to come and go pretty much as they pleased but regulated them strictly while they were on duty.

No matter how loose their structure, at least one truth
about the partisans generally held throughout the war: rebel

militia almost always got the best of their Tory counterparts. The reasons were many, but the primary one was the superiority of rebel leadership. Even some Tories admitted that they had no partisan leaders to equal Francis Marion and Thomas Sumter.[2]

David Fanning, now operating as a colonel of the loyalist militia in North Carolina, was one of the few Tories who proved to be a partisan commander "of the first rank,"[3] in the estimation of historian John Buchanan. In his new post, Fanning laid down this brief list of rules as a template for loyalist militias to follow.

≈

Rules and Regulations for the well governing [of] the loyal Militia of the Province of North Carolina:

1st. No person to be admitted a militia man until he takes the oath of Allegiance to his Majesty, which is always to be done before the senior officer of the Regiment on the spot[.]

2d. All persons once enrolled, in a Militia company, and having taken the oath above mentioned, will be considered as entitled to every privilege and protection of a British subject, [but] on being detected joining the Rebels, will be treated as a deserter, and traitor.

3d. Every militia man is to repair, without fail or excuse, except sickness, at the time appointed, to the place assigned by his Colonel or Capt. with his arms, and accoutrements, and is not to quit his company, on any pretence whatever, without the knowledge and permission of his Captain or commanding officer.

4th. The Colonel of every County has full power to call his Regiment together, and march them when necessary for his Majesty's service; the Captain of each company has also power to assemble his company, when any sudden emergency renders it necessary, and which he is to report as soon as possible to his Colonel.

5th. Mutual assistance is to be given on all occasions; but so it is impossible to give positive directions on this subject, it is left to the discretion of the Colonels of Regiments, who must be answerable that their reasons for not affording assistance when required are sufficient.

6th. When the Militia of different counties are embodied, the senior officer is to Command; Colonels of Regiments are immediately to determine, the present rank of their Captains, in which, regard is to be had to seniority of commission or service. In cases of vacancies, the Colonels may grant temporary commissions, till recourse can be had to the Commanding officer of the King's troops.

7th. The men are to understand, that in what relates to the service they are bound to obey all officers, though not immediately belonging to their own companies.

8th. Courts Martial may sit by the appointment of the Colonel or Commanding officer; and must consist for the trial of an officer, of all the officers of the Regiment [to which] he belongs, except the Colonel or Commanding officer, and for the trial of a Non Commissioned Officer or Private, of 2 Captains, 2 subalterns and 3 privates, the latter to belong to the same company as the person to be tried. The eldest Captain to preside and the sentence of the Court, to be determined by plurality of votes, and approved by the Commanding Officer.

9th. No Colonel is to supersede an officer without trial; but he may suspend him till he can be tried.

10th. Quitting camp without permission, disobedience of orders, neglect of duty, plundering, and all irregularities and disorder to be punished at the discretion of a Court Martial, constituted as above mentioned; and by the approbation of the Colonel or Commanding officer, who has power to pardon, or remit, any part of a punishment, but not to increase or alter it.

11th. Every man must take the strictest care of his arms, and ammunition; and have them always ready for service.

12th. When the Militia is not embodied, they are at all times to be attentive to the motions of the Rebels, and immediately to acquaint the nearest Officer of any thing he may discover, who is to communicate it to his Colonel or other Officers as may be requisite.

13th. It is the duty of every person professing allegiance to his Majesty to communicate to the Commanding Officer of the nearest British port any intelligence he can procure of the assembling or moving of any bodies of Rebels. Persons employed on this occasion shall always be paid.

14th. Colonels of Regiments may assemble any number of their men they think necessary to be posted in particular spots of their districts. Their time of service on these occasions is to be limited; and they are at the expiration to be relieved by others. Great care is to be taken that no partiality is shown, that each take an equal proportion of duty, for which purpose alphabetical rolls are to be kept, by which the men are to be warned. Every Captain, to keep an account of the number of days each man of his company serves.

~

The strict observance of the above regulations is strongly recommended as the best means of the King's faithful subjects['] manifest superiority over the rebel militia; and [of ensuring] them that success their zeal and spirit in the cause of their country entitles them to expect.

Head Quarters, Wilmington, 25 Sept. 1781

I thought proper to administer the following oath of Allegiance unto those people I was dubious of:
"I _____ do swear on the Holy Evangelists of Almighty God to bear true allegiance to our Sovereign Lord, King George the 3d ; and to uphold the same. I do voluntarily promise for

to serve as Militia, under any officers appointed over me; and that I will when lawfully warned by our said officers assemble at any place by them directed in case of danger, in the space of 8 hours. I will go with my arms and accoutrements in good order, to suppress any rebels or others, the King's enemies; that I will not at any time do, or cause to be done any thing prejudicial to his Majesty's government; or suffer any intercourse, or correspondence, with the enemies thereof; that I will make known any plot, or plots, any wise inimical to his Majesty's forces, or loyal subjects, by me discovered, to his Majesty's officers contiguous, and it shall not exceed six hours before the said is discovered, if health and distance permit. This I do solemnly swear and promise to defend in all cases, whatsoever. So help me, God!"

Notes

[1]David Fanning, *The Narrative of Colonel David Fanning, A Tory in the Revolutionary War with Great Britain* (New York: reprinted for Joseph Sabin, 1865), 24–27.

[2]John Buchanan, *The Road to Guilford Courthouse: The American Revolution in the Carolinas* (New York: John Wiley & Sons, 1997), 192.

[3]Ibid.

PART IV

"Lay Waste with Fire and Sword"

October 1780 – January 1781

Kings Mountain

From a pamphlet by Isaac Shelby [1]; from *Autobiography of a Revolutionary Soldier*,[2] by James Collins; and from *The Memoir of Major Thomas Young*[3]

In one hour, the tide of the American Revolution in the South—if not the entire war—turned dramatically and, as it turned out, conclusively. One hour on October 7, 1780, set off a chain of events that led, a little more than a year later, to Cornwallis's raising a white flag over the battlements at Yorktown. The rebels would lose more battles after this hour, but they would never again suffer a rout as they had at Camden or lose an entire army as they had at Charleston. In one hour, a bunch of rednecks from the back of beyond changed the course of history.

One hour was all the Overmountain Men needed to defeat Major Patrick Ferguson and his Tory troops, dug in at the top of Kings Mountain. Ferguson was a brilliant, if erratic, professional soldier with a long record of service. The son of a minor Scottish aristocrat, he had conceived and patented an improvement on the breechloading rifle that he hoped to make the standard firearm of the British army, going so far as to demonstrate the weapon for King George III at Windsor Palace. A protégé of Sir Henry Clinton's, Ferguson had remained with Cornwallis as "Inspector of Militia," charged with recruiting, training, and commanding all loyalist militia in the Carolinas.

Though he shared the same contempt for militia as his fellow British (and, it has to be said, Continental) officers, Ferguson was also known as one of the few who would take the time to discuss issues and plans with "colonials."[4] During the siege of Charleston, he was present with Tarleton's British Legion at Moncks Corner when dragoons assaulted some Tory women; Ferguson, alone among the legion's officers, called for the offenders to be summarily shot.

Ferguson, though, had a weakness for dramatic pronouncements and schemes on an epic and bloody scale, so much so that Cornwallis worried that "his ideas are so wild and sanguine . . . it would be dangerous to trust him with the conduct of any plan."[5] Yet after Camden, that is exactly what Cornwallis did, sending Ferguson west to protect his Lordship's left flank as he pushed into North Carolina. Ferguson followed his orders with zeal, launching a pursuit of the rebel militias fleeing for the mountains after Horatio Gates's disaster. When he could not catch them, he sent a message to one of their leaders, Isaac Shelby, threatening to bring "fire and sword" to the mountain settlements if the rebels did not immediately turn themselves in.

The mountain settlers, the people of the western waters (because they lived where the rivers ran west), the Overmountain people, America's first hillbillies—whatever they might be called, they were not people to respond meekly to threats. They had already defied British authority simply by living in the place where they did, which the British had declared off-limits to white settlers. Those who had not already fought the British as militia had spent years fighting the Cherokees. John Buchanan writes of the typical Overmountain Man, "If he survived falling trees, fever, snake bites, drowning, disease, backbreaking labor, blood poisoning, and the scalping knife, he rode into a fight a warrior for the ages."[6]

In 1823, Isaac Shelby wrote an account of what followed from Ferguson's threats. This came after the publication of some private letters between Shelby and fellow Overmountain leader John Sevier in which Shelby criticized Colonel William Campbell, who led a regiment of Virginia militia at Kings Mountain. Shelby by that time had been twice the governor of Kentucky and had turned down President James Monroe's invitation to become secretary of war. He died of a stroke only three years after his pamphlet was published.

The second and third accounts of the Battle of Kings Mountain come from the boy soldiers James Collins and Thomas Young, whose partisan bands joined the Overmountain Men as they chased Ferguson through the back country. Though still in their teens, both Collins and Young were by now seasoned veterans of partisan warfare, though neither had fought in any battle on the scale of Kings Mountain.

≈

From a pamphlet by Isaac Shelby

Upon the defeat of General Gates and the American army at the battle of Camden . . . the Southern states were almost entirely abandoned to the enemy. The intelligence of that disastrous affair . . . spread universal consternation and alarm. All the bodies of militia that were in arms through the country were compelled to fly before the enemy. Some of these detachments (part of which I commanded) fled towards the mountains, and were hotly pursued by Major Ferguson, of the British army, with a strong force. Failing in the attempt to intercept their retreat, he took post at Gilbert Town [now Rutherfordton, North Carolina]. At that place he paroled a prisoner (one Samuel Philips, a distant connection of mine), and instructed him to inform the officers on the Western waters that if they did not desist from their occupation [opposition] to the British arms, and take protection under his standard, he would march his army over the mountains, hang their leaders, and lay their country waste with fire and sword. Philips lived near my residence, and came directly to me with this intelligence. I then commanded the militia of Sullivan County, North Carolina [now in Tennessee]. In a few days I went fifty or sixty miles to see Colonel Sevier, who was the efficient commander of Washington County, North Carolina [also now in Tennessee], to inform him of the message I had received, and to concert with him measures for our defense. After some consultation, we determined to march with all the men we could raise and attempt to surprise Ferguson by attacking him in his camp, or at any rate before he was prepared for us. We accordingly appointed a time and place of rendezvous. It was known to us that some two or three hundred of the militia who had been under the command of Colonel [Charles] McDowell, and were driven by the success of the enemy from the lower country, were then on the Western waters, and mostly in the County of Washington. . . . I saw some of their officers before we parted; Colonel Sevier engaged to give notice to these refugees, and to bring them into our measure. On my part, I undertook to procure the aid and cooperation of Colonel William Campbell, of Washington County, Virginia, and the men of that county, if practicable.

Having made the arrangements with Sevier, I returned home immediately, and devoted myself to all the necessary operations for our intended enterprise. I wrote to Col. Campbell, informing him what Sevier and I had agreed on, and urged him to join us with all the men he could raise. This letter I sent express to him at his own house, forty miles distant, by my brother, Moses Shelby. Col. Campbell wrote me for answer that he had determined to raise what men he could and march down by Flower Gap, to the southern borders of Virginia, to oppose Lord Cornwallis when he approached that state. . . . Of this I notified Col. Sevier by an express on the next day, and immediately issued an order calling upon *all* the militia of the county to hold themselves in readiness to march at the time appointed. I felt, however, some disappointment at the reply of Col. Campbell. The Cherokee towns were not more than eighty or one hundred miles from the frontiers of my county, and we had received information that these Indians were preparing a formidable attack upon us in the course of a few weeks; I was, therefore, unwilling that we should take away the whole disposable force of our counties at such a time; and without the aid of the militia under Col. Campbell's command, I feared that we could not otherwise have a sufficient force to meet Ferguson. I therefore wrote a second letter to Col. Campbell, and sent the same messenger back with it immediately, to whom I communicated at large our view and intentions, and directed him to urge them on Col. Campbell. This letter and messenger produced the desired effect, and Campbell wrote me that he would meet us at the time and place appointed.

... The 25th day of September, 1780, at Watauga, [were] the time and place appointed for our rendezvous[.] Col. Sevier had succeeded in engaging for our enterprise Col. Charles McDowell and many of the refugees before mentioned—and when assembled our forces were as follows: Col. William Campbell with four hundred men from Washington County, Virginia; Col. John Sevier with two hundred and forty men from Washington County, North Carolina; Col. Charles Mc-Dowell with one hundred and sixty men from the counties of Burke and Rutherford, who had fled before the enemy to the Western waters; and two hundred and forty men from Sullivan County, North Carolina, under my command. On the next day, the 26th of the month, we began our march, crossed the mountains, and, on the 30th, were joined by Col. Benjamin Cleveland with three hundred and fifty men from the counties of Wilkes and Surry, North Carolina.

The little disorders and irregularities which began to prevail among our undisciplined troops created much uneasiness in the commanding officers—the Colonels commanding regiments. We met in the evening, and consulted about our future operations. It was resolved to send to headquarters [Gates's, in Hillsborough, North Carolina] for a general officer to command us; and that, in the meantime, we should meet in council every day to determine on the measures to be pursued, and appoint one of our own body to put them in execution. I was not satisfied with this course, as I thought it calculated to produce delay, when expedition and dispatch were all important to us. We were then [with]in sixteen or eighteen miles of Gilbert Town, where we supposed Ferguson to be. I suggested these things to the council, and then observed to the officers that we were all North Carolinians except Col. Campbell, who was from Virginia; that I knew him to be a man of good sense, and warmly attached to the cause of his country; that he commanded the largest regiment; and that if they concurred with me, we would, until a general officer should arrive from headquarters, appoint him to command us, and march immediately against the enemy. To this proposition some one or two said, "Agreed." No written minute or record was made of it. I made the proposition to silence the expectations of Col. McDowell to command us—he being the commanding officer of the district we were then in, and had commanded the armies of militia assembled in that quarter all the summer before against the same enemy. He was a brave and patriotic man, but we considered him too far advanced in life, and too inactive, for the command of such an enterprise as we were then engaged in. . . . Col. McDowell, who had the good of his country more at heart than any title of command, submitted to what was done; but observed, that as he could not be permitted to command, he would be the messenger to go to headquarters for the general officer. He accordingly started immediately, leaving his men under his brother, Major Joseph McDowell, and Col. Campbell assumed the chief command. He was, however, to be regulated and directed by the determinations of the Colonels, who were to meet in council every day.

On the morning after the appointment of Col. Campbell, we proceeded towards Gilbert Town, but found that Ferguson, apprised of our approach, had left there a few days before. On the next night it was determined, in the council of officers, to pursue him unremittingly, with as many of our troops as could be well armed and well mounted, leaving the weak horses and footmen to follow on as fast as they could. We accordingly started about light the next morning, with nine hundred and ten men, thus selected. Continuing diligently our pursuit all that day, we were joined at the Cowpens, on the 6th, by Col. James Williams of South Carolina, and several field officers, with about four hundred men. Learning from him the situation and distance of the enemy, we traveled all that night, and the next day, through heavy rains, and came up with them about three o'clock in the afternoon of the 7th of October. They were encamped on an eminence called King's Mountain, extending from east to west, which on its summit was about five or six hundred yards long, and sixty to seventy broad. Our men were formed for battle. . . . The men who had belonged to Col. McDowell's command, which had been considerably augmented on the march, formed a part of the right wing under Sevier. Col. Campbell's regiment and my own composed the center—his on the right, and mine on the left. The right wing or column was led by Col. Sevier and Major [Joseph] Winston; the left by Cols. Cleveland and Williams; and each of these wings was about as strong as Campbell's regiment and mine united. Our plan was to surround the mountain and attack the enemy on all sides.

In this order, and with this view, we marched immediately to the assault. The attack was commenced by the two center columns, which attempted to ascend at the eastern end of the mountain. The battle here became furious and bloody, and many that belonged to Sevier's column were drawn into the action at this point, to sustain their comrades. In the course of the battle we were repeatedly repulsed by the enemy, and driven down the mountain. In this succession of repulses and attacks, and in giving succor to the points hardest pressed, much disorder took place in our ranks; the men of my column, of Campbell's column, and [a] great part of Sevier's, were mingled together in the confusion of the battle. Towards the latter part of the action, the enemy made a fierce and gallant charge upon us, from the eastern summit of the mountain, and drove us near to the foot of it. The retreat was so rapid that there was great danger of its becoming a rout.

. . . Our men were soon rallied and turned back upon the enemy, who in a few minutes after we again came into close action with them, gave way. We gained the eastern summit of the mountain and drove those who had been opposed to us along the top of it, until they were forced down the western end about one hundred yards, in a crowd, to where the other part of their line had been contending with Cleveland and Williams, who were maintaining their ground below them. It was here that Ferguson, the British commander, was killed— and a white flag was soon after hoisted by the enemy, in token of surrender. They were ordered to throw down their arms, which they did, and surrendered themselves prisoners at our discretion. It was some time before a complete cessation of the firing, on our part, could be effected. Our men, who had been scattered in the battle, were continually coming up, and continued to fire, without comprehending in the heat of the moment what had happened; and some, who had heard that at [Colonel Abraham] Buford's defeat the British had refused quarter to many who asked it, were willing to follow that bad example [see "Buford's Quarter," pages 65-72]. Owing to these causes, the ignorance of some, and the disposition of others to retaliate, it required some time, and some exertion on the part of the officers, to put an entire stop to the firing. After the surrender of the enemy, our men gave spontaneously three loud and long shouts.

From *Autobiography of a Revolutionary Soldier*, by James Collins

At this time, there was [Elijah] Clarke, from Georgia, with his adherents, driven to take refuge in the confines of North Carolina. There was a communication between him and Moffitt. There were two parties of Tories posted on the west side of Broad River; one at a place called Black Stock, the other, lower down at a place called Musgrove's Mills. It was agreed that we should attack both places at the same time, if possible. It fell to our lot to attack at Black Stock, while Clarke was to attack Musgrove's; both parties succeeded in driving away the enemy. We had five men wounded—three badly though not mortally, the other two slightly; while Clarke had several wounded and one or two killed. What number the enemy lost I cannot say at this time, but they had several killed and wounded at both places. We all took care to secure what powder and balls we could in such cases, never encumbering ourselves with heavy plunder. As soon as the business was over, we fixed up our wounded as well as we could, and moved off. We had not proceeded far, till we fell in with a number of families, perhaps 50, or more, pushing on with all possible speed to take refuge in North Carolina. Some had wagons, some had packs, all the company being old men, women, and boys. We placed our wounded in some of the wagons, and guarded the whole until we got across Broad River; we then took the wounded and conveyed them to a place of safety, where they recovered. . . . In a few weeks our danger began to increase; Ferguson was coming on with his boasted marksmen, and seemed to threaten the destruction of the whole country. The Tories were flocking to his standard from every quarter, and there appeared little safety for us; but as God would have it, a patriotic party sprung up . . . under Colonels Campbell, Williams, Shelby, and Cleveland; Sevier, from the mountains, joined in, together with Hamright [Frederick Hambright], and some other leaders. As they advanced their numbers kept augmenting; our chance of safety was to join, if possible, the advancing patriots, to accomplish which, we passed on through North Carolina; but before we reached them, the army had passed. We fell in their rear, took their trail, and pushed on till we overtook them without being intercepted. It had been expected that Ferguson would cross Broad River, high up, and they would meet him on his march. But he had turned his course; took a road to the right, and steered more to the east, towards Charlotte in North Carolina, thus steering right through our section of country. Our army fell in his rear, at no great distance behind, and took his trail and commenced pursuit. The spies brought in news that he had crossed Broad River at a place called the Cherokee Ford, and had made a stand. He had taken a position at a small distance down the river, below the crossing place; having the river on one side, a high rocky ridge on the other, and a large old field fronting where we must of necessity cross the river. The pursuing army had not a single baggage wagon or any kind of camp equipage; everyone ate what he could get, and slept in his own blanket, sometimes eating raw turnips, and often resorting to a little parched corn, which by the by, I have often thought, if a man would eat a mess of parched corn and swallow two or three spoonfuls of honey, then take a good draught of cold water, he could pass longer without suffering than with any other diet he could use. On Friday evening, we came to the river, with the full expectation of meeting them, and being attacked in crossing; we passed over but no enemy appeared. The enemy had moved on, I think, about nine miles, and made a stand on a place called King's Mountain, and determined to give battle. We had encamped for the night, on the ground the enemy had left; on Saturday morning, October 7th, 1780, we were paraded, and harangued in a short manner, on the prospect before us. The sky was overcast with clouds, and at times a light mist of rain falling; our provisions were scanty, and hungry men are apt to be fractious; each one felt his situation; the last stake was up and the severity of the game must be played; everything was at stake—life, liberty, property, and even the fate of wife, children, and friends, seemed to depend on the issue; death or victory was the only way to escape suffering. Near two o'clock in the afternoon we came in sight of the enemy, who seemed to be fully prepared to give battle at all risks. When we came up, we halted, and formed in order of battle. Shelby happened to be in command that day as every colonel took command day about [by turns]. The men were disposed of in three divisions—the right was commanded by Cleveland and Sevier, the left by Campbell and Williams, and the center by Shelby and Hamright. The enemy was posted on a high, steep, and rugged ridge, or spur of the mountain, very difficult of access, with a small stream of water running on each side; along each stream was a narrow strip of flat ground. The plan was to surround the mountain and attack them on all sides, if possible. In order to do this, the left had to march under the fire of the enemy to gain the position assigned to them, on the stream on the right of the enemy, while the right was to take possession of the other stream; in doing this they were not exposed, the cliff being so steep as to cover them completely. Each leader made a short speech in his own way to his men, desiring every coward to be off immediately; here I confess I would willingly have been excused, for my feeling[s] were not the most pleasant—this may be attributed to my youth, not being quite 17 years of age—but I could not well swallow the appellation of coward. I looked around; every man's countenance seemed to change; well, thought I, fate is fate, every man's fate is before him and he has to run it out, which I am inclined to think yet. I was commanded this day by Major [William] Chronicle and Captain Watson. We were soon in motion, every man throwing four or five balls in his mouth to prevent thirst, also to be in readiness to reload quick. The shot of the enemy soon began to pass over us like hail; the first shock was quickly over, and for my own part, I was soon in a profuse sweat. My lot happened to be in the center, where the severest part of the battle was fought. We soon attempted to climb the hill, but were fiercely charged upon and forced to fall back to our first position; we tried a second time, but met the same fate; the fight then seemed to become more furious. Their leader, Ferguson, came in full view, within rifle shot as if to encourage his men, who by this time were falling very fast; he soon disappeared. We took to the hill a third time; the enemy gave way; when we had gotten near the top, some of our leaders roared out, "Hurrah, my brave fellows! Advance! They are crying for quarter!"

By this time, the right and left had gained the top of the cliff; the enemy was completely hemmed in on all sides, and no chance of escaping—besides, their leader had fallen. They soon threw down their arms and surrendered. After the fight was over, the situation of the poor Tories appeared to be really pitiable; the dead lay in heaps on all sides, while the groans of the wounded were heard in every direction. I could not help turning away from the scene before me, with horror, and though exulting in victory, could not refrain from shedding tears. "Great God!" said I, "Is this the fate of mortals, or was it for this cause that man was brought into the world?"

On examining the dead body of their great chief, it appeared that almost 50 rifles must have been leveled at him, at the same time; seven rifle balls had passed through his body, both of his arms were broken, and his hat and clothing were literally shot to pieces. Their great elevation above us had proved their ruin; they overshot us altogether, scarce touching a man, except those on horseback, while every rifle from below seemed to have the desired effect. In this conflict I had fired my rifle six times, while others had perhaps fired nine or 10. I had by this time learned to shoot a rifle pretty well, and was not a bad hand in the second class, and had come to this conclusion: never to retreat alone, shoot without an object, or lay down my gun until the last extremity; for, thought I, a gun, though empty, might keep an enemy at bay. Whether I effected anything or not is unknown to me. My first shot I ever doubted, for I really had a shake on me at the time; but that soon passed over, and I took the precaution to conceal myself as well as I could, behind a tree or rock, of which there were plenty, and take as good aim as possible.

Next morning, which was Sunday, the scene became really distressing; the wives and children of the poor Tories came in, in great numbers. Their husbands, fathers, and brothers, lay dead in heaps, while others lay wounded or dying; a melancholy sight indeed, while numbers of the survivors were doomed to abide the sentence of a court martial, and several were actually hanged. As regards the numbers that fell, authors have disagreed; yet none of [them] overrated the number. I know our estimate, at the time, was something over 300. We proceeded to bury the dead, but it was badly done; they were thrown into convenient piles, and covered with old logs, the bark of old trees, and rocks; yet not so as to secure them from becoming a prey to the beasts of the forest, or the vultures of the air; and the wolves became so plenty that it was dangerous for anyone to be out at night for several miles around; also, the hogs in the neighborhood gathered in to the place to devour the flesh of men, inasmuch as numbers chose to live on little meat rather than eat their hogs, though they were fat; half of the dogs in the country were said to be mad, and were put to death. I saw, myself, in passing the place, a few weeks after, all parts of the human frame, lying scattered in every direction. As God would have it, there had but few of our men been slain—15 or 16—but of that number some of our bravest men; Colonels Williams and Hamright, with Major Chronicle, and some other distinguished men, had fallen. These were buried in the flat ground under the hill, near where the battle commenced, and I expect their graves are to be seen there to this day.

Of the troop, or company, to which I belonged, we had two badly wounded; one, a lieutenant, by the name of Watson, the other, a private, named Caldwell; we carried them to their own homes, in the evening, where they both died, in a few days. Poor fellows! They were raised together, fought together, died nearly at the same time in the same house, and lie buried together. In the evening, there was a distribution made of the plunder, and we were dismissed. My father and myself drew two fine horses, two guns, and some articles of clothing, with a share of powder and lead; every man repaired to his tent, or home. It seemed like a calm, after a heavy storm had passed over, and for a short time, every man could visit his home, or his neighbor, without being afraid. After the result of the battle was known, we seemed to gather strength, for many that before lay neutral, through fear or some other cause, shouldered their guns, and fell in the ranks; some of them making good soldiers.

From *The Memoir of Major Thomas Young*

The next engagement I was in was at King's Mountain, S.C., I believe on the 7th of October, 1780. I was under the command of Colonel [Thomas] Brandon. Late in the evening preceding the battle, we met Colonels Campbell, Shelby, Cleveland, and Sevier, with their respective regiments, at the Cowpens, where they had been killing some beeves [cattle]. As soon as we got something to eat, for we were very hungry and weary, we retired to sleep at random in the woods. I did not wake until broad daylight. In the morning we received intelligence that Major Ferguson was encamped somewhere near the Cherokee Ford on Broad River. We pushed forward, but heard no tidings of the enemy. At a meeting house, on the eastern side of the river, we discovered some signs and continued our pursuit for some distance, when a halt was ordered, and were on the point of sending out for some beeves, when we met George Watkins, a Whig, who had been taken prisoner and was on his way home on parole. He gave us information of the position of the enemy. A consultation of the officers was then held, and the command was given to Colonel Campbell. Watkins had informed us that we were within a mile of the enemy. We then formed into four divisions; who commanded each division I cannot now say. I think Colonel [Benjamin] Roebuck commanded the one I was in.

Major Ferguson had taken a very strong position upon the summit of the mountain, and it appeared like an impossibility to dislodge him, but we had come there to do it, and we were determined, one and all, to do it, or die trying. The attack was begun on the north side of the mountain. The orders were at the firing of the first gun, for every man to raise a whoop, rush forward, and fight his way as he best could. When our division came up to the northern base of the mountain, we dismounted, and Colonel Roebuck drew us a little to the left and commenced the attack.

I well remember how I behaved. Ben Hollingsworth and I took right up the side of the mountain, and fought our way, from tree to tree, up to the summit. I recollect I stood behind one tree and fired till the bark was nearly all knocked off, and my eyes pretty well filled with it. One fellow shaved me pretty close, for his bullet took a piece out of my gun-stock. Before I was aware of it, I found myself apparently between my own regiment and the enemy, as I judged, from seeing the paper which the Whigs wore in their hats, and the pine knots the Tories wore in theirs, these being the badges of distinction.

On the top of the mountain, in the thickest of the fight, I saw Colonel Williams fall, and a braver or a better man never died upon the field of battle. I had seen him once before that day; it was in the beginning of the action, as he charged by me full speed around the mountain; toward the summit a ball struck his horse under the jaw when he commenced stamping as if he were in a nest of yellow jackets. Colonel Williams threw the reins over the animal's neck, sprang to the ground, and dashed onward. The moment I heard the cry that Colonel Williams was shot, I ran to his assistance, for I loved him as a father, he had ever been so kind to me, and almost always carried cake in his pocket for me and his little son Joseph. They carried him into a tent, and sprinkled some water in his face. He revived, and his first words were, "For God's sake, boys, don't give up the hill!" I remember it as well as if it had occurred yesterday. I left him in the arms of his son Daniel, and returned to the field to avenge his fall. Colonel Williams died next day, and was buried not far from the field of his glory.

Joseph Williams—who was a mere boy—and his brother Daniel, were, I think, subsequently massacred by the Tories at Hay's station. I remember to have heard it that they were surrounded by the Tories, and during the fight a crib or outhouse around the building in which the Whigs were stationed caught fire, and when they found there was no hope, Daniel Williams threw his father's pistols into the flames, exclaiming that he would rather see them burn, than go into the hands of a Tory. Our loss at the battle of King's Mountain was about 25 killed and wounded. The enemy lost above 300, who were left on the ground, among them Major Ferguson. We took, moreover, seven or eight hundred prisoners. Awful indeed was the scene of the wounded, the dying, and the dead on the field, after the carnage of that dreadful day.

A few days after the battle, a court martial was held to try some of the Tories who were known to be of the most outrageous and blood-thirsty character. About 20 were found guilty, but 10 received a pardon or respite. Nine were hung, and the 10th was pinioned, awaiting his fate. It was now nearly dark. His brother, a mere lad, threw his arms around him, and set up a most piteous crying and screaming, as if he would go into convulsions. While the soldiers were attracted by his behavior, he managed to cut the cords, and his brother escaped.

After the battle we marched upon the head waters of Cane Creek, in North Carolina, with our prisoners, where we all came very nearly starving to death. The country was very thinly settled, and provisions could not be had for love or money. I thought green pumpkins, sliced and fried, about the sweetest eating I ever had in my life. From this point we marched over into the Dutch settlements in the fork of Catawba and recruited, until we joined General [Daniel] Morgan at Grindal Shoals.

Notes

[1] Lyman C. Draper, *King's Mountain and Its Heroes: History of the Battle of King's Mountain, October 7th, 1780, and the Events Which Led to It* (Cincinnati, Ohio: Peter G. Thomson, Publisher, 1881), 562–66.

[2] James Potter Collins, *Autobiography of a Revolutionary Soldier*, revised and prepared by John M. Roberts (Clinton, La.: *Feliciana Democrat*, 1859), 49–54.

[3] Thomas Young, *The Memoir of Major Thomas Young* (Penfield, Ga.: *Orion* magazine, 1843).

[4] John Buchanan, *The Road to Guilford Courthouse: The American Revolution in the Carolinas* (New York: John Wiley & Sons, 1997), 203.

[5] Ibid., 202.

[6] Ibid., 207.

The Battle of the Cowpens

From General Daniel Morgan's report
to Nathanael Greene[1] and
from *The Memoir of Major Thomas Young*[2]

*Without Patrick Ferguson to protect his flank, and with the
"hornets" of Mecklenburg harassing his men's every move, Cornwallis left Charlotte in October to set up winter quarters in Winnsboro, South Carolina. Horatio Gates and what was left of the Continental Army in the Carolinas—fewer than 1,500 men present
and fit for duty—returned to Charlotte in his wake. The Overmountain Men returned to their homes to protect them against
possible Cherokee attack, while the partisans who had joined them
resumed their raids and skirmishes.*

*The disaster at Camden had convinced the Continental Con-
gress that their man Gates was not right for the job, and they left the
choice for his successor up to George Washington. Washington chose*

the man he had wanted all along: Nathanael Greene of Rhode Is-
land. Greene left Washington's command a week after the Battle of
Kings Mountain and started south, stopping along the way to beg
for reinforcements and supplies from Congress, Maryland, and
Virginia. Having received very little of either, he reached Charlotte
on December 2, 1780, virtually empty-handed. All he brought to
the beleaguered Continentals now under his command were his
keen eye for detail, his fighting instinct, his brilliance at organiza-
tion, and—finally—a strategic mastery to match Cornwallis's (see
"The Race to the Dan," pages 200-218).

If Greene was the strategist who could outthink Cornwallis,
the man who rode into Greene's headquarters the next day was the
battler who could outfight Cornwallis, Tarleton, or anyone else the
British could send against him. In an already eventful life, Daniel
Morgan had been a teenage runaway fending for himself on the
Virginia frontier, a notorious brawler, a prosperous wagoner, an
Indian fighter, and an accomplished soldier. John Buchanan de-
scribes him this way: "Renowned from Quebec to the Carolinas,
celebrated in one army and feared by another, his life a succession
of dramas one of which would be enough for most men, Brigadier
General Daniel Morgan of the Virginia Line was by far the Con-
tinentals' finest battle captain. If one were to judge him by all who
have led Americans into battle, he would have no superiors and
few peers."[3]

Morgan had first seen war as a wagoner pressed into service
during the French and Indian War, in the march that came to be
known as Braddock's Defeat. During the fighting, Morgan dumped
his cargo and—while many wagoners cut their horses from their
leads and hightailed it out—evacuated the wounded. Before that,
during the march itself, Morgan had argued with a British lieuten-

ant, who struck him with the flat of his sword. Morgan responded as any frontier brawler would, knocking the officer out with one punch. For this, he received 500 lashes, a punishment known to kill some men. But Morgan claimed for the rest of his life to have stayed conscious and counted each stroke.[4]

When the Revolutionary War started, Morgan organized a company of Virginia riflemen and made his name at the siege of Boston, the failed invasion of Canada, and especially the two American victories at Saratoga, where his elite riflemen so terrorized John Burgoyne's Indian scouts that they refused to depart camp, leaving the British blind. A congressional snub sent the proud Morgan home in 1779 (though Congress refused to accept his resignation); the onset of rheumatic sciatica kept him there. Bedridden for most of a year, and still awaiting a promised promotion to brigadier general, Morgan nonetheless set out for the Carolinas when Gates asked him to take command of the Southern Department's light troops. He did not reach Gates in time to help him at Camden, and it remains questionable if even Morgan's battlefield prowess could have salvaged that debacle.

Greene knew the resource he had in Morgan. Realizing that the Charlotte area was strategically vulnerable and stripped bare of supplies, Greene decided to move the bulk of his army to near Cheraw, South Carolina, from where he could monitor Cornwallis, rebuild his army, and prevent the British from supporting the loyalists there and in Cross Creek, North Carolina. Flying in the face of conventional military wisdom, though, Greene also decided to split his force, sending roughly 600 of his best cavalry and infantry west of the Catawba, under Morgan's command. Though less imaginative minds have carped, then and now, Greene had at least three very solid reasons for the split: one, living off the land would be easier for two smaller armies in two locations; two, Morgan's presence west of the Catawba stiffened Whig resolve in the back country; and, three, the divided army put Cornwallis in a strategic dilemma. If Cornwallis moved against Greene at Cheraw, Morgan could slip behind him to attack the British posts at Ninety-Six, South Carolina, and Augusta, Georgia. And if Cornwallis moved against Morgan, Greene could slip around him to attack Camden or even Charleston.

Morgan took with him some of the Continentals' finest fighters, including the cavalry of William Washington (a distant cousin of George's) and the veterans of the Maryland and Delaware lines under John Eager Howard and Robert Kirkwood. As he moved west, Morgan gathered more of the rebels' finest: North Carolina militia under William Lee Davidson and Georgia and South Carolina militia under Andrew Pickens—the third, behind Thomas Sumter and Francis Marion, of South Carolina's "Holy Trinity" of guerrilla warriors.[5] As 1780 turned into 1781, Morgan's forces were already scattering the Tories on Cornwallis's far western flank. The British commander knew he had to act fast, and knew he had no officer better at acting fast than Banastre Tarleton. Cornwallis sent Tarleton and his legion west with orders to hunt down and corner Morgan's force. Cornwallis would then follow Tarleton with reinforcements, and together they would smash Morgan and go after Greene. Cornwallis found himself delayed, though, waiting for his own reinforcements to keep Greene in check. And Tarleton was never one to wait when the enemy was in his view.

Morgan, once he knew Tarleton was on his trail, intended to cross the Broad River and leave South Carolina for the haven of the Thicketty Mountains in southwestern North Carolina before rejoining Greene. Tarleton proved too fast for him, though, and Morgan realized he would have to make a stand. He chose his ground at a place called the Cowpens.

A few days after the battle, Morgan sent the following report to Greene, in which he explained the circumstances that led to the battle, the action itself, and his brilliant and innovative disposition of his troops, the only "significant original tactical thought" produced by any general on either side of the American Revolution, in the view of John Buchanan.[6] Throughout the war, Continental generals had cursed Whig militia for their inability to stand firm against a British charge (see "A Narrative of the Battle of Camden," pages 101-16) and described them as cowards. Morgan, a son of the frontier, understood that militiamen were not cowards, but that they were being asked to do something they had not been trained to do. Morgan would ask them to do only what they could do, and no more.

Years after the battle, one of those militiamen, Thomas Young, described what Morgan asked of them, and the way he asked it. Young's account does more justice to Morgan's brilliant leadership than Morgan's own, and also provides a rare look at Morgan's opponent.

From General Daniel Morgan's report
to Nathanael Greene

Camp near Cane Creek, January 19th, 1781

Dear Sir:

The troops I have the honor to command have been so
fortunate as to obtain a complete victory over a detachment
from the British army, commanded by Lieutenant Colonel
Tarleton. The action happened on the 17th . . . about sunrise,
at the Cowpens. It, perhaps, would be well to remark, for the
honor of the American arms, that although the progress of
this corps [Tarleton's British Legion] was marked with burning and devastation, and although they waged the most cruel
warfare, not a man was killed, wounded, or even insulted, after
he surrendered. Had not Britons during this contest received
so many lessons of humanity, I should flatter myself that this
might teach them a little. But I fear they are incorrigible.

To give you a just idea of our operations, it will be necessary to inform you, that on the 14th . . . having received certain
intelligence that Lord Cornwallis and Lt. Col. Tarleton were
both in motion, and that their movements clearly indicated
their intentions of dislodging me, I abandoned my encampment on Grindall's Ford on the Pacolet, and on the 16th, in the
evening took possession of a post, about seven miles from the
Cherokee Ford, on Broad River. My former position subjected
me at once to the operations of Cornwallis and Tarleton, and
in case of a defeat, my retreat might easily have been cut off.
My situation at the Cowpens enabled me to improve any ad-

vantages I might gain, and to provide better for my own security should I be unfortunate. These reasons induced me to take this post, at the risk of its wearing the face of a retreat.

I received regular intelligence of the enemy's movements from the time they were first in motion. On the evening of the 16th . . . they took possession of the ground I had removed from in the morning, distant from the scene of action about 12 miles. An hour before daylight one of my scouts returned and informed me that Lt. Col. Tarleton had advanced within five miles of our camp. On this information, I hastened to form as good a disposition as circumstances would admit, and from the alacrity of the troops, we were soon prepared to receive him. The light infantry, commanded by Lieutenant Colonel Howard, and the Virginia militia under the command of Major [Frank] Triplett, were formed on a rising ground, and extended a line in front. The third regiment of dragoons, under Lieutenant Colonel Washington,[7] were posted at such a distance in their rear, as not to be subjected to the line of fire directed at them, and to be so near as to be able to charge the enemy should they be broken. The volunteers of North Carolina, South Carolina, and Georgia, under the command of the brave and valuable Colonel Pickens, were situated to guard the flanks. Major [Charles] McDowell, of the North Carolina volunteers, was posted on the right flank in front of the line, 150 yards; and Major Cunningham, of the Georgia volunteers, on the left, at the same distance in front. Colonels Brannon and [John] Thomas, of the South Carolinians, were posted in the right of Major McDowell, and Colonels [Joseph] Hays and [James] McCall, of the same corps, on the left of Major Cunningham. Captains Tate and Buchanan, with the Augusta riflemen, to support the right of the line.

The enemy drew up in single line of battle, 400 yards in front of our advanced corps. The first battalion of the 71st regiment was opposed to our right, the 7th regiment to our left, the infantry of the legion to our center, the light companies on their flanks. In front moved two pieces of artillery. Lieutenant Colonel Tarleton, with his cavalry, was posted in the rear of his line.

The disposition of battle being thus formed, small parties of riflemen were detached to skirmish with the enemy, upon which their whole line moved on with the greatest impetuosity, shouting as they advanced. McDowell and Cunningham gave them a heavy and galling fire, and retreated to the regiments intended for their support. The whole of Colonel Pickens's command then kept up a fire by regiments, retreating agreeably to their orders. When the enemy advanced to our line, they received a well-directed and incessant fire. But their numbers being superior to ours, they gained our flanks, which obliged us to change our position. We retired in good order about 50 paces, formed, advanced on the enemy, and gave them a fortunate volley, which threw them into disorder. Lieutenant Colonel Howard, observing this, gave orders for the line to charge bayonets, which was done with such address, that they fled with the utmost precipitation, leaving their field pieces in our possession. We pushed our advantages so effectually, that they never had an opportunity of rallying, had their intentions been ever so good.

Lieutenant Colonel Washington, having been informed that Tarleton was cutting down our riflemen on the left, pushed forward, and charged them with such firmness, that instead of attempting to recover the fate of the day, which one would have expected from an officer of his [Tarleton's] splendid character, broke and fled.

The enemy's whole force were now bent solely in providing for their safety in flight—the list of their killed, wounded, and prisoners, will inform you with what effect Tarleton, with the small remains of his cavalry, and a few scattering infantry he had mounted on his wagon horses, made their escape. He was pursued 24 miles, but owing to our having taken a wrong trail at first, we never could overtake him.

As I was obliged to move off of the field of action in the morning, to secure the prisoners, I cannot be so accurate as to the killed and wounded of the enemy as I could wish. From the reports of an officer whom I sent to view the ground, there were 100 non-commissioned officers and privates, and ten commissioned officers killed, and 200 rank and file wounded. We have now in our possession 502 non-commissioned officers and privates [as] prisoners, independent of the wounded, and the militia are taking up stragglers continually. Twenty-nine commissioned officers have fell into our hands. Their rank, etc., you will see by an enclosed list. The officers I have paroled; the privates I am conveying by the safest route to Salisbury.

Two standards, two field pieces, 35 wagons, a traveling forge, and all their music are ours. Their baggage, which was immense, they have in a great measure destroyed.

Our loss is inconsiderable, which the enclosed return will evince. I have not been able to ascertain Colonel Pickens's loss, but know it to be very small.

From our force being composed of such a variety of corps,

a wrong judgment may be formed of our numbers. We fought [having] only 800 men, two-thirds of which were militia. The British, with their baggage guard, were not less than 1150, and these veteran troops. Their own officers confess that they fought 1037.

Such was the inferiority of our numbers, that our success must be attributed to the justice of our cause and the bravery of our troops. My wishes would induce me to mention the name of every sentinel in the corps I have the honor to command. In justice to the bravery and good conduct of the officers, I have taken the liberty to enclose you a list of their names, from a conviction that you will be pleased to introduce such characters to the world.

Major [Edward] Giles, my aide, and Captain Brookes, my brigade-major, deserve and have my thanks for their assistance and behavior on this occasion.

The Baron de Gleabuch, who accompanies Major Giles with these dispatches, served with me in the action as a volunteer, and behaved in such a manner as merits your attention.

I am, dear sir, your obedient servant,

Daniel Morgan

From *The Memoir of Major Thomas Young*

We then returned to Morgan's encampment at Grindal Shoals, on the Pacolet, and there we remained, eating beef and scouting through the neighborhood until we heard of Tarleton's approach. Having received intelligence that Colonel Tarleton designed to cross the Pacolet at Easternood Shoals above us, General Morgan broke up his encampment early on the morning of the 16th, and retreated up the mountain road by Hancock's Ville, taking the left hand road not far above, in a direction toward the head of Thicketty Creek. We arrived at the field of the Cowpens about sundown, and were then told that there we should meet the enemy. The news was received with great joy by the army. We were very anxious for battle, and many a hearty curse had been vented against Gen. Morgan during that day's march, for retreating, as we thought, to avoid a fight.

Night came upon us, yet much remained to be done. It was all important to strengthen the cavalry. General Morgan knew well the power of Tarleton's legion, and he was too wily an officer not to prepare himself as well as circumstances would admit. Two companies of volunteers were called for. One was raised by Major [Benjamin] Jolly of Union District, and the other, I think, by Major McCall. I attached myself to Major Jolly's company. We drew swords that night, and were informed we had authority to press any horse not belonging to a dragoon or an officer into our service for the day. It was upon this occasion I was more perfectly convinced of General Morgan's qualifications to command militia than I had ever before been. He went among the volunteers, helped them fix their swords, joked with them about their sweet-hearts, told them to keep in good spirits, and the day would be ours. And long after I laid down, he was going about among the soldiers encouraging them, and telling them that the old Wagoner would crack his whip over Ben (Tarleton) in the morning, as sure as they lived. "Just hold up your heads, boys, three fires," he would say, "and you are free, and then when you return to your homes, how the old folks will bless you, and the girls kiss you, for your gallant conduct!" I don't believe he slept a wink that night!

But to the battle. Our pickets were stationed three miles in advance. Samuel Clowney was one of the picket guard, and I often heard him afterwards laugh at his narrow escape. Three of Washington's dragoons were out on a scout, when they came almost in contact with the advanced guard of the British army; they wheeled, and were pursued almost into camp. Two got in safely; one poor fellow, whose horse fell down, was taken prisoner. It was about day that the pickets were driven in. The morning of the 17th of January, 1781, was bitterly cold. We were formed in order of battle, and the men were slapping their hands together to keep warm—an exertion not long necessary. The battle field was almost a plain with a ravine on both hands, and very little undergrowth in front or near us. The regulars, under the command of Colonel Howard, a brave man, were formed in two ranks, their right flank resting upon the head of the ravine on the right. The militia were formed on the left of the regulars, under command of Colonel Pickens, their left flank resting near the head of the ravine on the left. The cavalry formed in rear of the center, or rather in rear of the left wing of the regulars. About sunrise, the British line advanced at a sort of trot, with a loud halloo. It was the most beautiful line I ever saw. When they shouted, I heard Morgan say, "They give us the British halloo, boys, give them the Indian halloo, by G--," and he galloped along the lines, cheering the men, and telling them not to fire until we could see the whites of their eyes. Every officer was crying, "Don't fire!" for it was a hard matter for us to keep from it. I should have said the British line advanced under cover of their artillery; for it opened so fiercely upon the center, that Colonel Washington moved his cavalry from the center towards the right wing. The militia fired first. It was, for a time, *pop-pop-pop*, and then a whole volley; but when the regulars fired, it seemed like one sheet of flame from right to left. Oh, it was beautiful! I have heard old Colonel Fair say often that he believed John Savage fired the first gun in this battle. He was riding to and fro, along the lines, when he saw Savage fix his eye upon a British officer; he stepped out of the ranks, raised his gun, fired, and he saw the officer fall. After the first fire, the militia retreated, and the cavalry covered their retreat. They were again formed and renewed the attack, and we retired to the rear. They fought some time, and retreated again and then formed a second time. In this I can hardly be mistaken, for I recollect well that the cavalry was twice, during the action, between our army and the enemy. I have understood that one of the retreats was ordered by mistake by one of Morgan's officers. How true this is I cannot say. After the second forming, the firing became general and unremitting. In the hottest of it, I saw Colonel [Thomas] Brandon coming at full speed to the rear and waving his sword to Colonel Washington. In a moment the command to charge was given, and I soon found that the British cavalry had charged the American right. We made a most furious charge, and cutting through the British cavalry, wheeled and charged them in the rear. In this charge, I exchanged my tackey [pony] for the finest horse I ever rode; it was the quickest swap I ever made in my life! At this moment the bugle sounded. We, about half-formed and making a sort of circuit at full speed, came up in rear of the British line, shouting and charging like madmen. At this moment Colonel Howard gave the word "charge bayonets!" and the day was ours. The British broke, and throwing down their guns and cartouche boxes, made for the wagon road, and did the prettiest sort of running!

After this Major Jolly and seven or eight of us resolved upon an excursion to capture some of the baggage. We went about 12 miles, and captured two British soldiers, two Negroes, and two horses laden with portmanteaus. One of the portmanteaus belonged to a paymaster in the British service, and contained gold. Jolly insisted upon my returning with the prize to camp, while he pursued a little farther. I did so. Jolly's party dashed onward, and soon captured an armorer's wagon, with which they became so much engaged that they forgot all about me. I rode along for some miles at my leisure, on my fine gray charger, talking to my prisoners, when, all at once I saw, coming in advance, a party, which I soon discovered to be British. I knew it was no time to consider now; so I wheeled, put spurs to my horse, and made down the road in hopes of meeting Jolly and his party. My horse was stiff, however, from the severe exercise I had given him that morning, and I soon found that they were gaining upon me. I wheeled abruptly to the right into a cross road, but a party of three or four dashed through the woods and intercepted me. It was now a plain case, and I could no longer hope to engage one at a time. My pistol was empty, so I drew my sword and made battle. I never fought so hard in my life. I knew it was death anyhow, and I resolved to sell my life as dearly as possible. In a few minutes one finger on my left hand was split open; then I received a cut on my sword arm by a parry which disabled it. In the next instant [I received] a cut from a sabre across my forehead, (the scar of which I shall carry to my grave,) the skin slipped down over my eyes, and the blood blinded me so that I could see nothing. Then came a thrust in the right shoulder blade, then a cut upon the left shoulder, and a last cut (which you can feel for yourself) on the back of my head—and I fell upon my horse's neck. They took me down, bound up my wounds, and placed me again on my horse a prisoner of war.

When they joined the party in the main road, there were two Tories who knew me very well—Littlefield and Kelly. Littlefield cocked his gun, and swore he would kill me. In a moment nearly 20 British soldiers drew their swords, and cursing him for a d----d coward, for wanting to kill a boy without arms and a prisoner, ran him off. Littlefield did not like me, and for a very good reason. While we were at Grindal Shoals with Morgan, he once caught me out, and tried to take my gun away from me. I knocked him down with it, and as he rose I clicked it, and told him if he didn't run I'd blow him through. He did not long hesitate which of the two to choose. I asked Kelly not to tell the British who I was, and I do not think the fellow did.

Colonel Tarleton sent for me, and I rode by his side for several miles. He was a very fine-looking man, with rather a proud bearing, but very gentlemanly in his manners. He asked me a great many questions, and I told him one lie, which I have often thought of since. In reply to his query whether Morgan was reinforced before the battle, I told him "he was not, but that he expected a reinforcement every minute." He asked me how many dragoons Washington had. I replied that "he had

70, and two volunteer companies of mounted militia, but you know they won't fight." "By G-d!" he quickly replied, "they did today, though!" I begged him to parole me, but he said if he did, I should go right off and turn to fighting again. I then told him he could get three men in exchange for me, and he replied, "Very well, when we get to Cornwallis's army, you shall be paroled or exchanged; and meanwhile, I'll see that your wounds are taken care of."

We got to Hamilton Ford, on Broad River, about dark. Just before we came to the river, a British dragoon came up at full speed, and told Colonel Tarleton that Washington was close behind in pursuit. It was now very dark, and the river was said to be swimming. The British were not willing to take water. Colonel Tarleton flew into a terrible passion, and drawing his sword, swore he would cut down the first man who hesitated. They knew him too well to hesitate longer. During the confusion, a young Virginian by the name of Deshaser (also a prisoner) and myself, managed to get into the woods. In truth a British soldier had agreed to let us escape, and to desert if we would assist him in securing the plunder he had taken. We slipped away one at a time up the river, Deshaser first, then myself. I waited what I thought a very long time for the British soldier, and he came not. At last I began to think the British were across, and I gave a low whistle—Deshaser answered me, and we met. It was now very dark and raining when we came to the Pacolet. I could not find the ford, and it was well, for the river was swimming. We therefore made our way up the river, and had not gone far before we approached a barn. It had a light in it, and I heard a cough. We halted and reconnoitered, and finding it occupied by some British soldiers, we pressed on and soon arrived at old Captain Grant's where I was glad to stop. The old man and his lovely daughter washed and dressed my wounds, and in looking over the bag of plunder which the soldier had given us, they found a fine ruffled shirt, which I put on and went to bed. I shall never forget that girl or the old man for their kindness!

On the next day I left with Deshaser, and arrived at home that evening, where I was confined by a violent fever for eight or ten day; but thanks to the kind nursing and attention of old Mrs. Brandon, I recovered. I now slept in the woods for about three weeks, waiting for some of the Whigs to come in and commence operations. I was concerned about a horse. The British soldiers, when they took me, dismounted me from the fine charger I captured at the Cowpens and put me on a pacing pony. One day I met old Molly Willard riding a very fine sorrel horse, and told her we must swap. She wouldn't listen to it, but I replied that there was no use in talking, the horse I would have, and the exchange was made not much to the old woman's satisfaction, for she didn't love the Whigs; I don't believe the Willards have forgiven me for that horse swap to this day.

NOTES

[1] James Graham, *The Life of General Daniel Morgan, of the Virginia Line of the Army of the United States, with Portions of His Correspondence* (New York: Derby & Jackson, 1856), 467–70.

[2] Thomas Young, *The Memoir of Major Thomas Young* (Penfield, Ga.: *Orion* magazine, 1843).

[3] John Buchanan, *The Road to Guilford Courthouse: The American Revolution in the Carolinas* (New York: John Wiley & Sons, 1997), 276.

[4]Ibid., 278.

[5]Greene had already told Marion, in essence, to keep doing what he had been doing—harassing the British in the Low Country. Sumter did not join Morgan in part because he was recovering from wounds and in part because he did not care to have another commanding officer in what he considered his turf.

[6]Buchanan, *The Road to Guilford Courthouse*, 316.

[7]William Washington was the cavalry commander who was bested twice by Tarleton during the siege of Charleston, at Moncks Corner and Leneuds Ferry.

PART V

"Then He Is Ours"
February — March 1781

The Battle of Cowan's Ford

From *Narrative of the Battle of Cowan's Ford*,[1]
by Robert Henry

Tarleton's defeat at the Cowpens began a fury of motion by both armies that would last into the spring. Tarleton—with precious few survivors—reached Cornwallis's camp at Turkey Creek the same day as the expected reinforcements. Cornwallis set off with about 2,500 men after Daniel Morgan, whom he assumed would try to hold the ground he had won south of the Broad River. But Morgan, who knew that his corps was no match for all of Cornwallis's army, was already in North Carolina, marching fast toward the east side of the Catawba.

Ignoring Sir Henry Clinton's orders to keep South Carolina secured above all else, Cornwallis chased Morgan into North Carolina and east toward the Catawba. Near the end of January, Cornwallis camped at Ramsour's Mill, where Whig militia had defeated their Tory counterparts less than a year before. Determined to catch Morgan and Nathanael Greene and destroy the Continental Army in the South, Cornwallis ordered all his army's baggage—extra supplies, tents, even the rum ration—burned, starting with his Lordship's own.

When word of this reached Greene, he is supposed to have said, "Then he is ours."[2]

On the first day of February, the British reached the west bank of the Catawba not far north of Charlotte. Greene had ridden hundreds of miles—alone in what was still dangerous territory— to meet with Morgan in what is now southern Iredell County, leaving the army at Cheraw in the command of General Isaac Huger. Greene sent Morgan's corps north and dispatched word back to Huger to join the two armies at Guilford Courthouse, where Greensboro now stands. He left General William Lee Davidson and about 800 North Carolina militia to slow Cornwallis's crossing. Davidson divided his men to cover the two fords Cornwallis was most likely to use—Beattie's and Cowan's[3]—and set his cavalry in the rear, both to reinforce whichever ford the British used and to patrol the bank in case Cornwallis sent his own horsemen in a surprise flanking maneuver.

Among the militia at Cowan's Ford was yet another teenage veteran, Robert Henry, who had survived a bayonet wound at Kings Mountain. He was attending school near his home in what is now Gaston County when word came that the British were on their way. After the war, Henry became a surveyor and lawyer. He not only left his own account of what happened at Cowan's Ford but recorded the story of one of his Tory neighbors who was on the other side of the river and the battle.

Now, I will give my own version of the transaction of Cornwallis crossing Catawba River at Cowan's Ford, 1st February, 1781. Robert Beatty, a lame man, had taken up a school near the Tuckaseegee Ford, and had taught two days, and was teaching the third, when news came to the schoolhouse that Cornwallis was camped at Forney's, about seven miles from the schoolhouse; that Tarleton was ranging through the country catching Whig boys to make musicians of them in the British army. The master instantly dismissed the scholars, directing them to go home and spread the news, and retired himself. I went home, and that night Moses Starret, Alexander Starret, George Gillespie, Robert Gillespie, and Charles Rutledge came to my father's! We lay out that night, and shortly before daylight [we were joined by] my brother, Joseph Henry, who had left the army to give the news, and had crossed Catawba at John Beattie's in a canoe; and when he left the army, it was expected that Cornwallis would cross the river at Tuckaseegee Ford. Early in the morning this company [Henry and his friends] crossed the river at Beattie's, about two miles below Tuckaseegee Ford, where we hid our canoe, stayed some time at Beattie's—then went up to the Tuckaseegee Ford, and the army was at Cowan's Ford. We went up the river to John Nighten's, who treated us well by giving us potatoes to roast, and some whisky to drink. We became noisy and mischievous. Nighten said we should not have any more whisky. I proposed to go to the camp at the Ford, if anyone would let me have a gun and ammunition. My brother said he would give me his; Charles Rutledge proposed also to accompany me if he had a gun and ammunition, when Moses Starret gave him his gun. When about to start, I gave Nighten a hundred-dollar Continental bill for a half a pint of whisky. My brother gave another bill of the same size for half a bushel of potatoes. We dispatched the whisky. Being thus equipped, we went to the Ford, which was about a mile and a half. When we arrived, the guard that was there, 30 in number, made us welcome; the officer of the guard told us that Cornwallis would certainly attempt to cross that night or early in the morning; that each one of the guard had picked their stands to annoy the British as they crossed, so that when the alarm was given they would not be crowded, or be in each other's way—and said we must choose our stands. He accompanied us—Charles Rutledge chose the uppermost stand, and I chose the lowest, next the getting-out place of the Ford; the officer observed, that he considered that Davidson had done wrong, for that the army should have been stationed at the Ford—instead of which it was encamped three-fourths of a mile off, and that some person acquainted in the neighborhood of Forney should watch the movements of Cornwallis's army, and immediately when they would attempt to march, to hasten to the river and give the alarm; then that Davidson's army might be in readiness to receive them; the river being in the situation that it was then in, and the army thus prepared to receive them, [the officer] said that Cornwallis and a million of men could not cross without cannon as long as our ammunition would last. This I thought was a large expression; but since I think he was correct. He mentioned to each man of the guard to go to his stand again and examine it, so that when the alarm was given, that there should be no mistakes then made. I went to mine, and was well pleased with it—for in shooting, if I would miss my first aim, my lead would range along the British army obliquely and still do damage, and that I could stand it until the British would come to a place the water was riffling over a rock, then it would be time to run away. I remember that I looked over the guard to see if there was any person with whom I was acquainted, and found none but Joel Jetton, and my lame schoolmaster, Robert Beatty, with my comrade, Charles Rutledge.

. . . Shortly after dark a man across the river hooted like an owl, and was answered; a man went to a canoe some distance off, and brought word from him that all was silent in the British camp. The guard all lay down with their guns in their arms, and all were sound asleep at daybreak, except Joel Jetton, who discovered the noise of horses in deep water. The British pilot, Dick Beal, being deceived by our fires, had led them into swimming water. Jetton ran to the Ford[;] the sentry being sound asleep, Jetton kicked him into the river, endeavored to fire his gun, but it was wet. Having discovered the army, [Jetton] ran to our fires, having a fine voice, cried "The British! The British!" and fired a gun. Then each man ran to his stand; when I got to my stand, I saw them red[coats], but thought from loss of sleep my eyes might be mistaken, [and] threw water into them; by the time I was ready to fire, the rest of the guard had fired. I then heard the British splashing and making a noise as if drowning. I fired, and continued firing until I saw that one on horseback had passed my rock in the river, and saw that it was Dick Beal moving his gun from his shoulder, I expected, to shoot me. I ran with all speed up the bank, and when at the top of it, William Polk's horse breasted me, and General Davidson's horse, about 20 or 30 feet before Polk's horse, and near to the water's edge. All being silent on both sides, I heard the report of a gun, at the water's edge, being the first gun fired on the British side, and which I thought Dick Beal had fired at me. That moment Polk wheeled his horse, and cried, "Fire away, boys; there is help at hand." Turning my eye round, designing to run away, I saw my lame schoolmaster, Beatty, loading his gun by a tree; I thought I could stand it as long as he could, and commenced loading. Beatty fired, then I fired, the heads and shoulders of the British being just above the bank; they made no return fire; silence still prevailed. I observed Beatty loading again; I ran down another load—when he fired, he cried, "It's time to run, Bob." I looked past my tree, and saw their guns lowered, and then straightened myself behind my tree. They fired and knocked off some bark from my tree.

In the meantime Beatty had turned from his tree, and a bullet hit him in the hip, and broke the upper end of his thigh bone; he fell, still hallowing for me to run. I then ran at the top of my speed about 100 yards, when a thought struck me that the British had no horsemen to follow me, and that Davidson's army would be down at the river, and a battle would take place. Whereupon I loaded my gun, and went opposite to the Ford, and chose a large tree, sat down by it, and fired about 50 yards at the British. They fired several guns toward the place where I was; but their lead did not come nearer to me than about two rods.

I will now account for the great difference between the number of the British killed and those wounded. . . . The water at the Ford was fully waist-band deep, and in many places much deeper, with a very heavy pressing current, and when a man was killed or badly wounded, the current immediately floated him away, so that none of them that were killed or badly wounded were ever brought to the shore; and none but those slightly wounded reached the bank; Colonel Hall fell at the bank. I account for the three British that were killed . . . in this way: Beatty, the lame schoolmaster, an excellent marksman, fired twice, at a distance of not more than 20 yards, at the British, after they had ascended the high banks, as before stated; and I fired twice about the same distance. I therefore think Beatty, being the best marksman, killed two, and I killed one.

. . . I will give an account of the balance of my route after firing the last time, as heretofore stated. I went down the river to John Beattie's, where we had left our canoe; there I found my company, the two Starrets, the two Gillespies, my brother Joseph, and my comrade Charles Rutledge. I returned the gun to my brother after counting the cartridges—found seven missing—therefore I had fired seven times, as I supposed. The company remained at Beattie's until the next morning; when we took our canoe to cross the river to the Lincoln side, it was proposed that we would go to James Cunningham's fish-trap, and see if there were any fish in it. When we arrived at the trap, there were 14 dead men lodged in it, several of whom appeared to have no wound, but had drowned. We pushed them into the water, they floated off, and went each to his own home. This is my version of that transaction.

Now, I will give the common report of it. I will begin with the report of Nicholas Gosnell, one of our neighbors, a Tory, who was in Cornwallis's army when they crossed the Catawba at Cowan's Ford. It was frequently repeated from the extraordinary language he used, and from his manner of expression—it is therefore better imprinted on my memory. I will endeavor to give it in his own language: "His Lordship chose Dick Beal for his pilot, as he well know'd the Ford, and a durned pretty pilot he was, for he suffered himself to be led astray by the Rebel fires, and then had to go down to the Ford afterwards; but if he did bad one way, he did good another, for he killed their damned Rebel General [William Davidson]. The Rebels were posted at the water's edge—there wasn't many on 'em; but I'll be durned if they didn't slap the wad to his Majesty's men suicidally for a while, for I saw 'em hollerin' and a-snortin' and a-drownin'—the river was full on 'em a-snortin', a-hollerin' and a-drownin' until his Lordship reached the off bank; then the Rebels made straight shirttails [ran], and all was silent. . . . And when he [Cornwallis] rose the bank he was the best dog in the hunt, and not a rebel to be seen." This is the Tory version of Cornwallis crossing [the] Catawba at Cowan's Ford.

The following is the report of every person who lived at or near the river between Cowan's Ford and Tuckaseegee Ford: That a great number of British dead were found on Thompson's fish-dam, and in his trap, and numbers lodged on brush, and drifted to the banks; that the river stunk with dead carcasses; that the British could not have lost less than 100 men on that occasion.

. . . Soldiers who were in Davidson's army . . . stated that when William Polk returned from the Ford, and reported the death of General Davidson, that some of the army had left, and the rest were in confusion; that Polk prudently marched them off, not being able to fight Cornwallis on equal terms.

NOTES

[1]Robert Henry, *Narrative of the Battle of Cowan's Ford, February 1st, 1781* (Greensboro, N.C.: D. Schenck, Sr., 1891), 8–14.

[2]Daniel W. Barefoot, *Touring North Carolina's Revolutionary War Sites* (Winston-Salem, N.C.: John F. Blair, Publisher, 1998), 275.

[3]The names of Beattie's Ford, Cowan's Ford, and other important crossing points like Tuckaseegee Ford and Sherrald's (or Sherrill's) Ford can still be found on maps of the Catawba Valley. Tuckaseegee Road and Beattie's Ford Road are in Charlotte; Cowan's Ford Dam is near Cornelius; and the town of Sherrill's Ford is in Catawba County. The fords themselves, though, no longer exist; all are submerged beneath the waters of Lake Norman.

The Race to the Dan

From Memoirs of the War in the Southern
Department of the United States,[1]
by General Henry "Light Horse Harry" Lee

With Cornwallis across the Catawba, Nathanael Greene knew he had to keep his army out of British reach until he was ready to strike. His goal was to cross the Dan River into Virginia, where he could find rest, resupply, and reinforcement. If he could reach the Dan before Cornwallis did, he could not only gather his strength for a pitched battle but also exhaust the British troops and stretch their supply lines dangerously thin. For both armies, the next few weeks would bring near-constant marching, a chase that would come to be called the Race to the Dan.

Greene and Daniel Morgan's light corps pushed hard to the next river to be crossed: the Yadkin. The closest crossing point was the Trading Ford, just north of Salisbury. Winter rains had swollen the Yadkin so that only horses could use the ford, but here Greene's genius for organization and planning began to show. Even before his arrival in Charlotte, he had sent officers to thoroughly scout the Yadkin and the other major rivers of the North Carolina Piedmont. He had also instructed his quartermaster general, Edward Carrington, to procure all available boats and have them waiting at the Trading Ford. Greene used them to transport his infantry and baggage across the Yadkin, leaving Cornwallis without the means to follow in force. The British cannonaded the Continentals camped on the far bank but could not reach them.

Cornwallis marched his men along the Yadkin to the next crossing, the Shallow Ford, west of the Moravian town of Salem, while Greene and Morgan rendezvoused with the rest of their army at Guilford Courthouse. His army now intact, though still unready to face Cornwallis, Greene set his sights on the Dan. The easiest route would have been toward the upper reaches of that river, which were said to be easily fordable, but that would have put Greene's army dangerously close to Cornwallis's.

Greene now had his own legion, a light corps of cavalry and infantry as fast as the British Legion, commanded by an officer as bold as Banastre Tarleton: Henry "Light Horse Harry" Lee. Such a legion would prove useful during this final, frantic stage of the strategic withdrawal from the Carolinas, because Greene— exhibiting his usual diligence and foresight—had a plan.

Light Horse Harry was 24 years old during the Race to the Dan. Like William R. Davie, he was a graduate of the College of New Jersey. Lee had been commissioned a captain of Virginia cavalry in 1776. While serving in the Northeast, he became a close friend of George Washington's. In fact, it was Lee who would characterize Washington as "first in war, first in peace, and first *in the hearts of his countrymen." Though after the war Lee served as governor of Virginia, his later life was marked more by failure than success. While imprisoned for debt in 1808 and 1809, Lee began writing his* Memoirs of the War in the Southern Department of the United States, *first published in 1812. Though he may have lacked a head for business, Lee showed the same flair for writing that he had for warfare. The following account is taken from an 1870 republication, edited by one of Light Horse Harry's adoring sons, General Robert E. Lee.*

The inhabitants of this region of the state were well affected to the American cause, and General Greene had flattered himself with an expectation of here drawing around him reinforcements, which, with the light troops under Morgan, would enable him to hold Lord Cornwallis back for some days. But the fall of [William Lee] Davidson, and the rencounter [skirmish] at Terrant's Tavern,[2] disappointed, in their effect, this fond calculation. He dispatched orders to Brigadier [Isaac] Huger to relinquish the route to Salisbury, and to take the direct course to Guilford Courthouse, to which point he pressed forward with the light corps under Morgan. Passing through Salisbury, he proceeded to the trading ford on the Yadkin, where he arrived on the night of the second of February.

General Greene having withdrawn his troops from Beattie's Ford, on his Lordship's passage below, Lieutenant Colonel Webster and his division crossed the Catawba without opposition, and in the course of the day joined the British general.

Cornwallis had now gained one of the great roads leading to Salisbury, and the pursuit of our light troops was renewed with activity.

General Greene passed the Yadkin during the night of, and [on the] day following, his arrival at that river. The horse forded the stream, the infantry and most of the baggage were transported in flats. A few wagons fell into the hands of the enemy; for, notwithstanding the unfavorable condition of the roads and weather, Brigadier [Charles] O'Hara pressed forward with the British van, and overtook our rear guard. The retreating corps was again placed in a critical situation, and heaven was again propitious. The rain continued during the night; the Yadkin became unfordable; and Greene had secured all the flats on its northern bank.

The British general was a second time delayed by an unforeseen event. Relinquishing his anxious wish to bring the light troops to action before their junction with the main body, he recurred [resorted] to his last expedient, that of cutting Greene off from the upper fords of the Dan, and compelling his united force to battle, before he could either reach Virginia, or derive any aid from that state. With this view, he moved up the Yadkin to fords which were still passable. There his Lordship crossed; and, directing his course to the Dan, held Greene on his right, with a determination to throw the American general on the lower Dan, which the great fall of rain had rendered impassable without the assistance of boats, which he supposed unattainable. This object, his last hope, the British general pursued with his accustomed rapidity.

Greene was neither less active, nor less diligent. Continuing on the direct road to Guilford Courthouse, he reached that place on the 7th of February. Brigadier Huger, who had been overtaken by the Legion of Lee, arrived on the same day. The united force of Greene, including 500 militia, exceeded 2300; of which, 270 were cavalry of the best quality. The army of Cornwallis was estimated at 2500; but his cavalry, although more numerous than that of his adversary, was far inferior in regard to the size, condition, and activity of the horses. Taking into view his comparative weakness, General Greene determined to continue his retreat to Virginia. The British general was 25 miles from Guilford Courthouse; equally near with Greene to Dix's Ferry on the Dan, and nearer to the upper shallows or points of that river, which were supposed to be fordable, notwithstanding the late swell of water. Lieutenant Colonel [Edward] Carrington, quartermaster-general, suggested the propriety of passing at Irwin's Ferry, 70 miles from Guilford Courthouse, and 20 below Dix's. Boyd's Ferry was four miles below Irwin's, and the boats might be easily brought down from Dix's to assist in transporting the army at these near and lower ferries. The plan of Lieutenant Colonel Carrington was adopted, and that officer was charged with the requisite preparations. The route of retreat being determined, the place of crossing designated, and measures taken for the collection of boats, General Greene formed a light corps, consisting of some of his best infantry under Lieutenant Colonel [John Eager] Howard, of [William] Washington's cavalry, the Legion of Lee, and a few militia riflemen, making in all 700. These troops were to take post between the retreating and the advancing army, to hover round the skirts of the latter, to seize every opportunity of striking in detail, and to retard the enemy by vigilance and judicious positions: while Greene, with the main body, hastened toward the Dan, the boundary of his present toils and dangers.

The command of the light corps was offered to Brigadier Morgan, whose fitness for such service was universally acknowledged, and whose splendid success had commanded the high confidence of the general and army. Morgan declined the arduous task; and being at that time afflicted, as he occasionally was, with rheumatism, intimated a resolution of retiring from the army. Greene listened with reluctance to the excuse, and endeavored to prevail on him to recede from his determination. Lieutenant Colonel Lee, being in habits of intimacy with Morgan, was individually deputed [assigned] to persuade him to obey the universal wish. Many commonplace arguments were urged in conversation without success. Lee then represented that the brigadier's retirement at that crisis might induce an opinion unfavorable to his patriotism, and prejudicial to his future fame; that the resignation of a successful soldier at a critical moment was often attributed, and sometimes justly, to an apprehension that the contest would ultimately be unfortunate to his country, or to a conviction that his reputation had been accidentally acquired, and could not survive the vicissitudes of war. These observations appeared to touch the feelings of Morgan: for a moment he paused; then discovered a faint inclination to go through the impending conflict; but finally returned to his original decision. His refusal of the proffered command was followed by a request to retire, which was granted.

Colonel [Otho Holland] Williams, of Maryland, an accomplished gentleman and experienced soldier, being called to the station, so anxiously, but vainly pressed on Morgan, accepted it with cheerfulness, and diffidence. This last arrangement being finished, Greene put his army in motion, leaving Williams on the ground. The greater the distance between the main body and the light troops, the surer would be Greene's retreat. Williams, therefore, soon after breaking up from Guilford Courthouse, on the 10th, inclined to the left [west], for the purpose of throwing himself in front of Lord Cornwallis. This movement was judicious, and had an immediate effect. His Lordship, finding a corps of horse and foot close in front, whose strength and object were not immediately ascertainable, checked the rapidity of his march to give time for his long extended line to condense.

Could Williams have withdrawn himself from between Greene and Cornwallis, he might, probably, by occultly [secretly] reaching the British rear, have performed material service. Although his sagacity discovered the prospect, yet his sound judgment could not adopt a movement which might endanger the retreat of the army, whose safety was the object of his duty, and indispensable to the common cause. He adhered, therefore, to the less dazzling, but more useful system; and fastened his attention, first on the safety of the main body, next on that of the corps under his command; risking the latter only (and then without hesitation) when the security of Greene's retreat demanded it. Pursuing his course obliquely to the left, he reached an intermediate road; the British army being on his left and in his rear, the American in front and on his right. This was exactly the proper position for the light corps, and Williams judiciously retained it.

The enemy persevering in his rapid advance, our rear guard,

(composed of the Legion of Lee) and the British van under Brigadier O'Hara, were in sight during the day. Throughout the night, the corps of Williams held a respectable distance, to thwart, as far as was practicable, the nocturnal assault.

The duty, severe in the day, became more so at night; for numerous patrols and strong pickets were necessarily furnished by the light troops, not only for their own safety, but to prevent the enemy from placing himself, by a circuitous march, between Williams and Greene. Such a maneuver would have been fatal to the American army; and, to render it impossible, half of the troops were alternately appropriated every night to duty: so that each man, during the retreat, was entitled to but six hours' repose in 48. Notwithstanding this privation, the troops were in fine spirits and good health; delighted with their task, and determined to prove themselves worthy [of] the distinction with which they had been honored. At the hour of three, their toils were renewed; for Williams always pressed forward with the utmost dispatch in the morning, to gain such a distance in front as would secure breakfast to his soldiers, their only meal during this rapid and hazardous retreat. So fatigued was officer and soldier, and so much more operative is weariness than hunger, that each man not placed on duty surrendered himself to repose as soon as the night position was taken. Situated as was Williams, no arrangement could have been devised better calculated to effect the great object of his trust, and to secure food once a day to his troops.

The moment Lord Cornwallis found it necessary to change his course and to push for Dix's Ferry, he ordered his van to proceed slowly; and separating from it at the head of the main body, which had now arrived at a causeway leading to the desired route, he quickly gained the great road to Dix's Ferry, the course of the American light corps.

In pursuance of his system, Williams made a rapid morning's march; and leaving small patrols of cavalry near the enemy, sent forward the staff to select ground and prepare fires. The officers and dragoons, who had been necessarily kept in sight of the British, upon joining, were hastened in front to a farm house near the road, where they enjoyed, although a few hours later, a more comfortable meal. Lieutenant Carrington, who commanded the dragoons near the enemy's van, reported from time to time, in conformity to custom, by which it appeared that Cornwallis was moving as usual. The morning was cold and drizzly; our fires, which had been slow in kindling, were now lively; the meat was on the coals, and the corn-cake in the ashes. At this moment, a friendly countryman appeared, riding in haste to our camp, whither he had been directed by the sergeant of one of the horse patrols, with which he fell in on his way. The hurry of his approach, and the tired condition of his meager pony, evinced sincerity of heart; while the joy of his countenance declared his participation of interest. Asking for "the general," he was conducted to Colonel Williams, whom he bluntly informed that Lord Cornwallis, leaving his former route, had got into our road; that one half hour past he left the British army advancing, then only four miles behind; that accidentally discovering it from his field, where he was burning brushwood, he ran home, took the first horse he could find, and hastened to give his friends intelligence, which he deemed important. To attach doubt to the information of an honest-looking farmer would have violated all the rules of physiognomy. Williams always delighted to indulge and comfort his brave troops; and although he credited the countryman, was unwilling to interrupt their hasty repast. He therefore ordered Lieutenant Colonel Lee to detach from his cavalry, in order to ascertain the correctness of the intelligence. Captain [Mark] Armstrong, with one section of the horse, was dispatched accordingly, with the countryman for his guide. Soon after their departure, Carrington, still near the enemy, communicated the unusually slow progress of the vanguard. Combining this intelligence with that just received, Williams ordered Lieutenant Colonel Lee to strengthen Armstrong, and to take upon himself the command entrusted to that officer. Lieutenant Lewis, with the required addition, attended Lee, who dispatched one of the dragoons to overtake Armstrong, with orders directing him to move slowly until he should join. Quickly reaching Armstrong, who had not advanced more than a mile, Lee proceeded, in conformity with the advice of the countryman, two miles further; but seeing no enemy, he began to believe that his guide, however well affected, was certainly in a mistake. He determined, therefore, to return to breakfast, and leave Armstrong with three dragoons and the guide to proceed on to the spot, where the countryman's information had placed the enemy one hour before. Armstrong selected the dragoons mounted on the swiftest horses, and was in the act of moving, when the amicable countryman protested against accompanying him, unless furnished with a better horse. While with the whole detachment, he had thought himself safe, and never manifested any unwillingness to proceed; but now, being associated with the most alert of alert dragoons, whose only duty was to look and fly, he considered his danger extreme. This remonstrance, the justice of which could not be resisted, added another reason for crediting the information. Lee dismounted his bugler, whose horse was given to the countryman; and the bugler was sent back to camp to inform Williams how far the lieutenant colonel had proceeded without seeing any portion of the enemy, and of his intention to return after advancing Armstrong still further in front. Not doubting that the countryman had seen the British army, but supposing him to be mistaken in the distance, Lee led his detachment into the woods, and retired slowly, in sight of the road. He presumed, that should Armstrong be followed, the enemy would discover the trail of advancing horse in the road, and be deterred from a keen pursuit, which he did not wish to encourage, as it might deprive the light troops of their meal; although he was disposed in that event to seize any advantage which might offer. Not many minutes elapsed before a discharge of musketry announced that Armstrong had met the enemy; and shortly after[ward] the clangor of horses in swift speed declared the fast approach of cavalry. Armstrong soon appeared, closely followed by a troop of Tarleton's dragoons. Lee saw his captain and small party well in front, and hard in hand [riding hard]. For them he felt no apprehension; but for the safety of his bugler, on the countryman's pony, every feeling of his heart became interested. Being passed unperceived by the pursued and pursuers, Lee continued in the woods, determined to interpose in time to rescue his bugler, yet wishing the enemy to take the utmost allowable distance, that they might be deprived of support. Directing one of his lieutenants to halt with the rear file and ascertain whether additional cavalry was following, he hastened his progress, and soon saw the enemy's near approach to his defenseless bugler, who was immediately unhorsed, and sabered several times while prostrate on the ground. Lee was pressing forward to the road in the enemy's rear, when the officer who had been left behind rejoined with the acceptable information that no reinforcement was approaching. Gaining the road, the lieutenant colonel rushed forward in quick charge, and fell upon the troop of Tarleton soon after it had reached his bugler. Captain Miller [of Tarleton's cavalry] instantly formed, and fronted his approaching adversary; but his worn-down ponies were as ill calculated to withstand the stout, high-conditioned, active horses opposed to them, as were the intoxicated, inexpert riders unfit to contend with dragoons always sober, and excelling in horsemanship. The enemy was crushed on the first charge: most of them were killed or prostrated; and the residue, with their captain, attempted to escape. They were pursued by Lieutenant Lewis, who was commanded by Lee to give no quarters. This sanguinary mandate, so contrary to the American character, proceeded from a view of the bugler—a beardless, unarmed youth, who had vainly implored quarter, and in the agonies of death presented a spectacle resistless in its appeal for vengeance. Having placed the much wounded, hapless boy in the arms of the stoutest of his dragoons, and directed another soldier to attend them to camp, the lieutenant colonel proceeded in support of Lewis. Soon this officer was met, returning with Captain Miller, and all, save two, of the fugitives. The British captain was unhurt, but his dragoons were severely cut in the face, neck, and shoulders. Lewis was reprimanded on the spot for disobedience of orders; and Miller, being peremptorily charged with the atrocity perpetrated in his view, was told to prepare for death. The captain, with some show of reason, asserted that intelligence being his object, it was his wish and interest to save the soldier; that he had tried to do so, but his dragoons being intoxicated, all his efforts were ineffectual. He added that in the terrible slaughter under Lieutenant Colonel [Abraham] Buford [see "Buford's Quarter," pages 65-72], his humanity was experienced, and had been acknowledged by some of the Americans who escaped death on that bloody day. Lee was somewhat mollified by this rational apology, and was disposed to substitute one of the prisoners; but soon overtaking the speechless, dying youth, whose relation to his supporting comrade of the tragical particulars of his fate, when able to speak, confirmed his former impressions, he [Lee] returned with unrelenting sternness to his first decision. Descending a long hill, he repeated his determination to sacrifice Miller in the vale through which they were about to pass; and handing him a pencil, desired him to note on paper whatever he might wish to make known to his friends, with an assurance that it should be transmitted to the British general, At this moment, the rear guard communicated, by pistol discharge, the approach of the British van. Miller and his fellow prisoners were hurried on to Colonel Williams, who was at the same time informed of the enemy's advance. Williams put his corps in motion, and forwarded the captured officers and soldiers to headquarters, ignorant of the murder of the bugler, and the determination of Lieutenant Colonel Lee. Thus Miller escaped the fate to which he had been doomed, in order to convince the British cavalry under Lieutenant Colonel Tarleton that American blood should no longer be wantonly shed with impunity. Believing himself indebted for his life to the accident just recited, Captain Miller took care to represent, by letter, to his friends in the

British army, what had happened, and his conviction of what would have followed; and never afterward were such cruelties repeated by the British cavalry acting against the army of Greene.

. . . The pursuit was continued with unceasing activity. Williams[,] retiring in compact order, with the Legion of Lee in his rear, held himself ready to strike, whenever an opportunity presented. The skillful enemy never permitted any risk in detail, but preserved his whole force for one decisive struggle.

Having continued on the route to Dix's Ferry as far as he deemed advisable, and presuming that General Greene would on the next day reach the vicinity of the Dan, Colonel Williams determined to pass to the road on his right, leading to Irwin's Ferry, the route of the main body. He communicated his intention to the rear officer, and moved forward with increased celerity, for the purpose of gaining a distant night position, that he might be able to diminish the guards necessary for the security of his corps when close to the enterprising enemy.

Lieutenant Colonel Lee, having discovered, from conversation with his guides, that a byway in front would lead him into Williams's rear before the close of the evening, and save a considerable distance, determined to avail himself of the accommodation. A subaltern's [subordinate's] command of dragoons was left to proceed on the route taken by Colonel Williams, with order to communicate any extraordinary occurrence to the commandant [Williams] and to Lieutenant Colonel Lee. The cavalry, who met Miller in the morning, had lost their breakfast; and Lee's chief object in taking the short course was to avail himself of an abundant farm for the refreshment of his party. As soon as he reached the proposed route, the infantry were hastened forward, with directions to halt at the farm, and prepare for the accommodation of the corps; while the cavalry continued close to the enemy. In due time afterward, they were drawn off and passed through the woods, leaving in front of the British van the detachment which had been selected to follow the route of the light troops. The obscurity of the narrow road taken by Lee lulled every suspicion with respect to the enemy, and a few vedettes [mounted sentries] only were placed at intermediate points, rather to give a notice when the British should pass along than to guard the Legion from surprise. This precaution was most fortunate; for it so happened that Lord Cornwallis, having ascertained that Greene had directed his course to Irwin's Ferry, determined to avail himself of the nearest route to gain the road of his enemy, and took the path which Lee had selected. Our horses were unbridled, with abundance of provender before them; the hospitable farmer had liberally bestowed his meal and bacon, and had given the aid of his domestics in hastening the much-wished repast. To the surprise and grief of all, the pleasant prospect was instantly marred by the fire of the advanced vedettes—certain signal of the enemy's approach. Before the farm was a creek, which, in consequence of the late incessant rains, could be passed only by a bridge, not more distant from the enemy than from our party. The cavalry being speedily arrayed, moved to support the vedettes, while the infantry were ordered, in full run, to seize and hold the bridge.

The enemy was equally surprised with ourselves at this unexpected meeting, and the light party in front halted, to report and be directed. This pause was sufficient. The bridge was gained, and soon passed by the corps of Lee. The British followed. The road over the bridge leading through cultivated fields for a mile, the British army was in full view of the troops of Lee as the latter ascended the eminence, on whose summit they entered the great road to Irwin's Ferry.

Thus escaped a corps, which had been hitherto guarded with unvarying vigilance, whose loss would have been severely felt by the American general, and which had been just exposed to imminent peril from the presumption of certain security. Criminal improvidence! A soldier is always in danger, when his conviction of security leads him to dispense with the most vigilant precautions.

Cornwallis, at length in Greene's rear, urged his march with redoubled zeal, confident of overtaking his adversary before he could reach the Dan. Adverse efforts to accelerate and to retard were unceasingly exhibited during the evening; the enemy's van being sometimes so close as to indicate a determination to force the light troops to prepare for defense. Avoiding a measure replete with peril, Williams persevered in his desultory retreat. More than once were the Legion of Lee and the van of O'Hara within musket-shot, which presented so acceptable an invitation to the marksmen flanking the Legion that they were restrained with difficulty from delivering their fire. This disposition being effectually checked, the demeanor of the hostile troops became so pacific in appearance that a spectator would have been led to consider them members of the same army. Only when a defile [narrow passage] or a watercourse crossed our route did the enemy exhibit any indication to cut off our rear; in which essays, being always disappointed, their useless efforts were gradually discontinued.

The fall of night excited pleasure, as it promised respite

from toil. But illusory was the expectation, for the British general was so eager to fall on Greene, whom he believed within his grasp, that the pursuit was not intermitted. The night was dark, the roads deep, the weather cold, and the air humid. Williams, throwing his horse in front, and the infantry of the Legion in the rear, continued his retreat.

About eight in the evening, numerous fires discovered an encampment before us. No pen can describe the heart-rending feelings of our brave and wearied troops. Not a doubt was entertained that the descried camp was Greene's; and our dauntless corps were convinced that the crisis had now arrived when its self-sacrifice could alone give a chance of escape to the main body. With one voice was announced the noble resolution to turn on the foe, and by dint of desperate courage, so to cripple him as to force a discontinuance of pursuit. This heroic spirit, first breathed in whispers, soon gained the ear of Williams; who, alike daring and alike willing to offer up his life for the safety of an army on which the hopes of the South rested, would have been foremost in the bold conflict. But his first impressions soon yielded to conclusions drawn from a reference to the date of General Greene's last letter, which demonstrated the mistaken apprehension of the troops. Enjoying the delight inspired by their manly ardor, and commending their devotion to their country, he [Williams] calmed their disquietude. They shortly reached the camp of fires, and discovered that it was the ground where Greene had halted on the evening of the 11th. Relieved from the dire foreboding, the light corps continued its march until the rear officer made known to the commandant that the enemy had halted. The first convenient spot was occupied for the night; the fires were instantly kindled; the cold and wet, the cares and toils of the day, were soon forgotten in the enjoyment of repose.

About midnight our troops were put in motion, in consequence of the enemy's advance on our pickets, which the British general had been induced to order, from knowing that he was within 40 miles of the Dan, and that all his hope depended on the exertions of the following day. Animated with the prospect of soon terminating their present labors, the light troops resumed their march with alacrity. The roads continued deep and broken, and were rendered worse by being encrusted with frost; nevertheless, the march was pushed with great expedition. In the forenoon, one hour was applied by both commanders to the refreshment of their troops.

About noon Colonel Williams received a letter from General Greene, communicating the delightful tidings of his passage over the Dan on the preceding day. The whole corps became renovated in strength and agility; so powerful is the influence of the mind over the body. The great object of their long and faithful labor being so nearly accomplished, a general emulation [desire] pervaded all ranks to hasten to the boundary of their cares and perils. The hopes of the enemy were still high, and he rivaled our increased celerity, the van of O'Hara following close on the rear of Lee. About three in the evening we arrived within 14 miles of the river, and Colonel Williams, leaving the Legion of Lee to wait on the enemy, took the nearest course to Boyd's Ferry. Before sunset he gained the river, and was soon transported to the opposite shore.

Lee, at the assigned period, directed his infantry to follow on the route of Williams; and about dark withdrew with his cavalry, the enemy being still in motion. Between the hours of eight and nine, the cavalry reached the river, just as the boats had returned from landing the Legion infantry. In obedience to the disposition of Lieutenant Colonel Carrington, quartermaster general, who superintended, in person, his arrangements for the transportation of the army, the horses were turned into the stream, while the dragoons, with their arms and equipments, embarked in the boats. Unluckily, some of the horses turned back, and gaining the shore, fled into the woods; and for a time some apprehensions were entertained that they might be lost. They were, however, recovered, and being forced into the river, followed their fellows. In the last boat, the quartermaster general, attended by Lieutenant Colonel Lee and the rear troop, reached the friendly shore.

In the evening Lord Cornwallis had received the unwelcome news of Greene's safe passage over the Dan; and now, relinquishing his expectation of annihilating a second army, and despairing of striking the light corps, so long in his view and always safe, he gave repose to his vainly wearied troops.

Thus ended, on the night of the 14th of February, this long, arduous, and eventful retreat.

NOTES

[1] Henry Lee, *Memoirs of the War in the Southern Department of the United States* (New York: University Publishing Company, 1870), 234–47.

[2] At Terrant's (or Tarrant's) Tavern south of Salisbury, Tarleton and his legion caught up with some panicked militia, who tried to surrender after token opposition. True to his reputation, Tarleton butchered them.

The Battle of Guilford Courthouse

From *Memoirs of the War in the Southern Department of the United States,*[1] by General Henry "Light Horse Harry" Lee

Once again, Cornwallis found himself on one side of a river and Nathanael Greene safely on the other. His troops exhausted by the Race to the Dan, Cornwallis withdrew to Hillsborough, North Carolina, and raised the royal standard, hoping for an influx of Tory militia. They came, but in far fewer numbers than expected.

The British now found themselves hundreds of miles from their nearest base, at Camden. They had burned their supplies at Ramsour's Mill. No reinforcement was available. In fact, Cornwallis had not written to Sir Henry Clinton since he left South Carolina in January; the British high command had no idea where Cornwallis and his men were.

Greene, meanwhile, was resting his troops in Halifax County,

Virginia, where he could gather provisions, supplies, and reinforcements. In early March, Greene decided his army was ready to reengage Cornwallis's, if not in a pitched battle, then at least by harassing its flanks and rear. He had no intention of leaving the Carolinas to the British, even in their exhausted state. He sent Light Horse Harry Lee's legion back across the Dan and soon followed with the rest of the Continental Army in the South.

The armies and their attached partisans skirmished for the next two weeks as the generals sought to feel out their opponents and bring them to battle on their own terms. Finally, with the upper Piedmont stripped bare, Cornwallis left his camp at Spring Garden on the morning of March 15 determined to crush the Continentals once and for all. Greene deployed his men, in much the same formation Daniel Morgan had used at the Cowpens, astride the Spring Garden Road where it reached Guilford Courthouse.

Guilford Courthouse, erected near the great state road, is situated on the brow of a declivity, which descends gradually with an undulating slope for about a half mile. It terminates in a small vale, intersected by a rivulet. On the right of the road is open ground with some few copses of wood until you gain the last step of the descent, where you see thick glades of brushy wood reaching across the rivulet; on the left of the road from the courthouse a deep forest of lofty trees, which terminates nearly in a line with the termination of the field on the opposite side of the road. Below this forest is a small piece of open ground, which appeared to have been cultivated in corn the preceding summer. This small field was long, but narrow, reaching close to the swamp bordering upon the rivulet.

In the road Captain [Anthony] Singleton was posted, in a line with the termination of the large field and the commencement of the small one, with two six-pounders within close shot of the rivulet, where the enemy, keeping the road, would pass. Across the road on his left, some few yards in his rear, the North Carolina militia were ranged, under Generals [John] Butler and [Thomas] Eaton. At some distance behind this line, the Virginia militia, led by the Generals [Edward] Stevens and [Robert] Lawson, were formed in a deep wood; the right flank of Stevens and the left flank of Lawson resting on the great road. The Continental infantry, consisting of four regiments, were drawn up in the rear of the Virginia militia, in the field to the right of the road; the two regiments of Virginia, conducted by Colonel [John] Green and Lieutenant Colonel [Samuel] Hawes, under the order of Brigadier [Isaac] Huger, composing the right; and the two of Maryland, led by Colonel [John] Gunby, and Lieutenant Colonel [Benjamin] Ford, under the orders of Colonel [Otho Holland] Williams, composing the left. Of these, only the regiment of Gunby was veteran; the three others were composed of new soldiers, among whom were mingled a few who had served from the beginning of the war; but all the officers were experienced and approved. Greene, well informed of his enemy's inferiority in number, knew he could present but one line, and had therefore no reserve; considering it injudicious to weaken either of his lines by forming one. On the right, Lieutenant Colonel [William] Washington, with his cavalry, the old Delaware company, under the brave Captain [Robert] Kirkwood, and Colonel [Charles] Lynch, with a battalion of Virginia militia, was posted, with orders to hold safe that flank. For the same purpose, and with the same orders, Lieutenant Colonel Lee was stationed on the left flank with his Legion and the Virginia riflemen commanded by Colonel [William] Campbell.

In the rear line our small park [of artillery] was placed, with the exception of two sixes with Captain Singleton, who was now with the front line, but directed to repair to the rear as soon as the enemy should enter into close battle, and there take his assigned station.

As soon as the British van appeared, Singleton opened a cannonade upon it, convincing Lord Cornwallis of his proximity to the American army. Lieutenant [John] McCleod, commanding the royal artillery, hastened up with two pieces, and stationing himself in the road near the rivulet, returned our fire. Thus the action commenced: the British general in the meantime arranging his army in order of battle. Although he could form but one full line, he took the resolution of attacking an able general advantageously posted, with a force more than double, a portion whereof he knew to be excellent, supported by cavalry of the first character. Yet such was his condition, that Lord Cornwallis was highly gratified with having it in his power, even on such terms, to appeal to the sword. The 71st, with the regiment of [Carl von] Bose, formed his right, under the order of Major General [Alexander] Leslie; his left was composed of the 23rd and 33rd regiments, led by Lieutenant Colonel [James] Webster.

The royal artillery, directed by Lieutenant McCleod, and supported by the light infantry of the guards and the jagers [Hessian riflemen], moved along the road in the center. The first battalion of guards, under Lieutenant Colonel [Chapel]

Norton, gave support to the right; while Brigadier [Charles] O'Hara, with the grenadiers and second battalion of guards, maintained the left. Lieutenant Colonel Tarleton, with the cavalry in column, formed the reserve on the road, in the rear of the artillery.

The moment the head of the British column passed the rivulet, the different corps, in quick step, deployed to the right and left, and soon were ranged in line of battle.

Leslie instantly advanced upon the North Carolina militia. These troops were most advantageously posted under cover of a rail fence, along the margin of the woods; and Campbell's riflemen and the Legion infantry connected in line with the North Carolina militia, turning with the fence as it approached the rivulet, raked by their fire the right of the British wing, entirely uncovered; the Legion cavalry, in the woods, in a column pointing to the angular corner of the fence ready to support the militia on its right, or the infantry of the Legion to its left. The appearance in this quarter was so favorable, that sanguine hopes were entertained by many of the officers, from the manifest advantage possessed, of breaking down the enemy's right before he approached the fence; and the troops exhibited the appearance of great zeal and alacrity.

Lieutenant Colonel Webster took his part with his usual ability, moving upon the Virginia militia, who were not so advantageously posted as their comrades of North Carolina, yet gave every indication of maintaining their ground with obstinacy. Stevens, to give efficacy to this temper, and stung with the recollection of their inglorious flight in the battle of Camden, had placed a line of sentinels in his rear, with orders to shoot every man that flinched. When the enemy came within long shot, the American line, by order, began to fire. Undismayed, the British continued to advance; and having reached a proper distance, discharged their pieces and rent the air with shouts. To our infinite distress and mortification, the North Carolina militia took to flight, a few only of Eaton's brigade excepted, who clung to the militia under Campbell; which, with the legion, manfully maintained their ground. Every effort was made by the Generals Butler and Eaton, assisted by Colonel Davie, commissary general, with many of the officers of every grade, to stop this unaccountable panic; for not a man of the corps had been killed, or even wounded. Lieutenant Colonel Lee joined in the attempt to rally the fugitives, threatening to fall upon them with his cavalry. All was vain; so thoroughly confounded were these unhappy men, that, throwing away arms, knapsacks, and even canteens, they rushed like a torrent headlong through the woods. In the meantime the British right became so injured by the keen and advantageous contest still upheld by Campbell and the Legion, as to render it necessary for Leslie to order into line the support under Lieutenant Colonel Norton, a decided proof of the difficult condition to which he must have been soon reduced, had the North Carolina militia done their duty. The chasm in our order of battle, produced by this base desertion, was extremely detrimental in its consequences; for, being seized by Leslie, it threw the corps of Lee out of combination with the army, and also exposed it to destruction. General Leslie, turning the regiment of Bose, with the battalion of guards, upon Lee, pressed forward himself with the 71st to cover the right of Webster, now keenly engaged with the Virginia militia; and seized the most advantageous position, which he preserved throughout the battle. Noble was the stand of the Virginia militia; Stevens and Lawson, with their faithful brigades, contending for victory against the best officer in the British army, at the head of two regiments distinguished for intrepidity and discipline; and so firmly did they maintain the battle (secured on their flank by the position taken by Washington, who, anxious to contribute to the aid of his brave countrymen, introduced Lynch's battalion of riflemen upon the flank of Webster, already fully engaged in front), that Brigadier O'Hara, with the grenadiers and the second battalion of the guards, were brought into the line in support of Webster. As soon as this assistance was felt, Lieutenant Colonel Webster, turning the 33rd upon Lynch, relieved his flank of all annoyance; and instantly O'Hara, advancing with the remainder of the left wing with fixed bayonets, aided by the 71st under Leslie, compelled, first Lawson's brigade, and then Steven[s]'s, to abandon the contest. Unhappily, the latter general received a ball through his thigh, which accelerated not a little the retreat of his brigade. The militia no longer presented even the show of resistance; nevertheless, such had been the resolution with which the corps under Lee, sustaining itself on the left against the first battalion of guards and the regiment of Bose, and so bravely did the Virginia militia support the action on the right, that, notwithstanding the injurious desertion of the first line without exchanging a shot, every corps of the British army, except the cavalry, had been necessarily brought into battle, and many of them had suffered severely. It cannot be doubted, had the North Carolina militia rivaled that of Virginia upon this occasion, that Lord Cornwallis must have been defeated; and even now, the Continental troops being in full vigor, and our cavalry unhurt, there was good ground to expect victory.

Persevering in his determination to die or conquer, the British general did not stop to concentrate his force, but pressed forward to break our third line. The action, never intermitting on his right, was still sternly maintained by Colonel Norton's battalion of guards and the regiment of Bose, with the rifle militia and the Legion infantry; so that this portion of the British force could not be brought to bear upon the third line, supported by Colonel Washington at the head of the horse, and Kirkwood's Delaware company. General Greene was well pleased with the present prospect, and flattering himself with a happy conclusion, passed along the line, exhorting his troops to give the finishing blow. Webster, hastening over the ground occupied by the Virginia militia, sought with zeal the Continental line, and presently approached its right wing. Here was posted the first regiment of Maryland, commanded by Colonel Gunby, having under him Lieutenant Colonel [John Eager] Howard. The enemy rushed into close fire; but so firmly was he received by this body of veterans, supported by Hawes's regiment of Virginia and Kirkwood's company of Delawares (being weakened in his contest with Stevens's brigade, and, as yet unsupported, the troops to his right not having advanced, from inequality of ground or other impediments), that with equal rapidity he was compelled to recoil from the shock.

Recrossing a ravine in his rear, Webster occupied a[n] advantageous height, waiting for the approach of the rest of the line. Very soon Lieutenant Colonel [James] Stuart, with the first battalion of guards, appeared in the open field, followed successively by the remaining corps, all anxious to unite in the last effort. Stuart, discovering Ford's regiment of Maryland on the left of the first regiment, and a small copse of wood concealing Gunby, pushed forward upon Ford, who was strengthened by Captain [Ebenezer] Finley with two six-pounders. Colonel Williams, commanding the Maryland line, charmed with the late demeanor of the first regiment, hastened toward the second, expecting a similar display, and prepared to combine his whole force with all practicable celerity; when, unaccountably, the second regiment gave way, abandoning to the enemy the two field pieces.

Gunby[,] being left free by Webster's recession, wheeled to his left upon Stuart, who was pursuing the flying second regiment. Here the action was well fought; each corps manfully struggling for victory; when Lieutenant Colonel Washington, who had, upon the discomfiture of the Virginia militia, placed himself upon the flank of the Continentals, agreeably to the order of battle, pressed forward with his cavalry.

Stuart beginning to give ground, Washington fell upon him sword in hand, followed by Howard with fixed bayonets, now commanding the regiment in consequence of Gunby being dismounted. This combined operation was irresistible. Stuart fell by the sword of Captain Smith, of the first regiment; the two field pieces were recovered; his battalion driven back with slaughter, its remains being saved by the British artillery, which to stop the ardent pursuit of Washington and Howard, opened upon friends as well as foes; for Cornwallis, seeing the vigorous advance of these two officers, determined to arrest their progress, though every ball leveled at them must pass through the flying guards. Checked by this cannonade, and discovering one regiment passing from the woods on the enemy's right, across the road, and another advancing in front,

Howard[,] believing himself to be out of support, retired, followed by Washington.

To these two regiments (which were the 71st, which General Leslie had so judiciously conducted after the ignominious flight of the North Carolina militia, and the 23rd, the right of Webster) Brigadier O'Hara, though grievously wounded, brought the remnant of the first battalion of guards, whom he in person rallied; and, with the grenadiers, filled up the interval between the left and right wing.

Webster, the moment Stuart appeared in the field, putting Ford to flight, recrossed the ravine and attacked Hawes's regiment of Virginia, supported by Kirkwood's company. The action was renewed in this quarter with vigor; the 71st and 23rd, connected in their center by the first battalion and grenadiers of the guards, having at the same time moved upon Howard. Meanwhile the long-impending contest upon the enemy's right continued without intermission; each of the combatants getting gradually nearer to the flanks of their respective armies, to close with which was the desired object of both. At length Lieutenant Colonel Norton, with his battalion of guards, believing the regiment of Bose adequate to the contest, and close to the great road to which he had been constantly inclining, pressed forward to join the 71st. Relieved from this portion of the enemy, Lieutenant Colonel Lee dispensed with his cavalry, heretofore held in the rear to cover retreat in case of disaster, ordering it to close with the left of the Continental line, and there to act until it should receive further orders. Upon Bose the rifle and Legion infantry now turned with increased animation, and with confidence of success. Major De Buy, of the regiment of Bose, continued to defend himself with obstinacy; but pressed as he was by superior force, he at length gave ground, and fell back into the rear of Norton. Still annoying him with the rifle corps under Campbell, Lee hastened with his infantry to rejoin his cavalry upon the flank of the Continentals, the point so long and vainly contended for. In his route, he found the battalion of guards under Norton in possession of the height first occupied by Lawson's brigade of Virginia militia. With this corps, again the Legion infantry renewed action; and supported by the van company of the riflemen, its rear still waiting upon Major De Buy, drove it back upon the regiment of Bose. Every obstacle now removed, Lee pressed forward, followed by Campbell, and joined his horse close by Guilford Courthouse.

Having seen the flight of the second regiment of Maryland, preceded by that of the North Carolina militia, the corps of Lee severed from the army, and considering it, if not destroyed, at least thrown out of battle by Leslie's judicious seizure of the interval produced by the panic of the North Carolina militia, and in all probability not able to regain its station in the line—Greene, immutable in the resolution never to risk annihilation of his force, and adverting to [considering] his scanty supply of ammunition, determined, when he found all his personal efforts, seconded by Colonels Williams and [Edward] Carrington, to rally the second regiment of Maryland nugatory [futile], to provide for retreat. Colonel Green, one of the bravest of brave soldiers, with his regiment of Virginia, was drawn off without having tasted of battle, and ordered to a given point in the rear for the security of this movement. Had General Greene known how severely his enemy was crippled, and that the corps under Lee had fought their way to his Continental line, he would certainly have continued the conflict; and in all probability would have made it a drawn day, if not have secured to himself the victory. Ignorant of these facts, and finding Webster returned to battle—O'Hara, with his rallied guards in line—and General Leslie, with the 71st connected with them on the right, and followed, as he well knew, by the remnant of his wing—he [Greene] persevered in his resolution, and directed a retreat, which was performed deliberately under cover of Colonel Green. General Huger, who had, throughout the action, given his chief attention to the regiment of Hawes, the only one of the two constituting his brigade ever engaged, and which, with Kirkwood's company, was still contending with Lieutenant Colonel Webster, now drew it off by order of the general; while Colonel Williams effected the same object in his quarter; both abandoning our artillery, as their horses had been mostly killed; and General Greene preferred leaving his artillery, to risking the loss of lives in drawing them off by hand. Just after this had taken place, Lieutenant Colonel Lee joined his cavalry at the courthouse; and, unpursued, retired down the great Salisbury road, until a crossroad enabled him to pass over to the line of retreat. The 71st and 23rd regiments, supported by the cavalry of Tarleton, followed our army with the show of falling upon it; but the British general soon recalled them, and General Greene, undisturbed, was left to pursue his retreat. He halted first three miles from the field of battle, to collect stragglers and fugitives, and afterward retired leisurely to his former position at the iron works.

The pertinacity [persistence] with which the rifle corps of Campbell and the Legion infantry had maintained the battle on the enemy's right induced Lord Cornwallis to detach the British horse to that quarter. The contest had long been ebbing before this corps arrived; and Lieutenant Colonel Tarleton found only a few resolute marksmen in the rear of Campbell, who continued firing from tree to tree. The appearance of cavalry determined these brave fellows to retire and overtake their corps.

Thus the battle terminated. It was fought on the 15th of March, a day never to be forgotten by the southern section of the United States. The atmosphere calm, and illumined with a cloudless sun; the season rather cold than cool; the body braced and the mind high-toned by the state of the weather. Great was the stake, willing were the generals to put it to hazard, and their armies seemed to support with ardor the decision of their respective leaders.

NOTES

[1]Henry Lee, *Memoirs of the War in the Southern Department of the United States* (New York: University Publishing Company, 1870), 275–83.

PART VI

Endgame
September 1781 – December 1782

The Battle of Eutaw Springs

By Nathanael Greene, in a letter to Congress[1]

In the late spring of 1781, when Cornwallis moved north, Greene moved south and commenced the reconquest of South Carolina. He first attempted to surprise the British garrison at Camden, commanded now by the young Francis, Lord Rawdon, but Rawdon was alerted and drove the Americans back at Hobkirk's Hill. British losses in the battle, though, were far greater than the Americans', and Rawdon was soon forced to abandon Camden.

Greene sent Light Horse Harry Lee and Francis Marion against British outposts at Fort Motte, Fort Granby (now Columbia), and Georgetown, all of which fell to the Americans. He then sent Lee and Andrew Pickens to take the British forts at Augusta, Georgia, one of them commanded by Thomas "Burnfoot" Browne (see "The Making of a Tory Partisan," pages 28-36). After a defense that would have been heroic had the Tories won the war, Augusta fell, too. Greene, meanwhile, laid siege to the last British outpost, at Ninety-Six, but was forced to withdraw when he learned that British reinforcements had arrived in Charleston and that Rawdon was on his way to Ninety-Six with 2,000 men.

Lee, Marion, Thomas Sumter, and Pickens continued to harass the British and Tories for the rest of the summer, while Greene regrouped his Continentals at the High Hills of the Santee. In September, Greene felt his army was ready to take the field again. He met the British army, marching north from Charleston, at Eutaw Springs.

The Battle of Eutaw Springs would turn out to be the last major engagement of the Revolutionary War in the Carolinas, though partisan warfare continued for more than a year. It would also turn out like every other battle Nathanael Greene fought: a costly victory for his opponent. For all of Greene's strategic brilliance, he never won a single battle as overall commander. Greene had his faults as a general; as author Michael Stephenson notes, "What he lacked as a field commander was Morgan's understanding of the common soldier, his inspirational presence, and, crucially, Morgan's nerve: the instinct to go for the coup de grâce."[2] One cannot help wondering what would have happened at Guilford Courthouse, Hobkirk's Hill, Ninety-Six, and Eutaw Springs if Morgan had been able to continue the campaign.

Despite Greene's record, his achievement in the Carolinas cannot be overestimated. The Rhode Island Quaker who taught himself military strategy by reading the classics of history and theory, the soldier who entered the Continental line as a private and ended as Washington's choice to succeed him as commander in chief, did *as much as anyone—including Washington himself—to win the American Revolution.*

Greene sent the following report to Congress after the Battle of Eutaw Springs. Almost all of the heroes of the Revolutionary War in the Carolinas served under Greene during this final battle: William Washington, Light Horse Harry Lee, Otho Holland Williams, Thomas Sumter, Francis Marion, Andrew Pickens, William Richardson Davie. These officers had survived the fall of Charleston, the rout at Camden, the bleak summer of 1780, the savagery of the guerrilla war in the back country, the rigors of the Race to the Dan. They had survived without giving up hope, and their hope was about to be rewarded.

~

Gen. Greene to the President of Congress
Near Ferguson's Swamp, Sept. 11, 1781

In my dispatches of the 25th of August, I informed your Excellency that we were on the march to Friday's Ferry, with the intent of forming a junction with the troops of the State and a corps of militia that were assembled, and to attack the English army, encamped near M'Leod's Ferry.

On the 27th, upon our arrival there, I received advice that the enemy had retired. We passed the river at Howell's Ferry, and our first post was Motte's plantation, where I learnt that the enemy had stopped at Eutaw Springs, about forty miles from us, where they had received a reinforcement, and they prepared to establish a post there. To dislodge them, I determined to hazard an engagement, although we were considerably inferior in number.

We began to march on the 5th of September; and we advanced by small marches, as well to disguise our intention, as to give time to General Marion, who had been detached, to rejoin us; so that it was the 7th when we came to Bendell's plantations, within seventeen miles of the enemy.

We marched to attack the enemy at four o'clock in the morning of the 8th. Our front line was composed of four small battalions of militia, two of North and two of South Carolina; our second line consisted of three small brigades of Continental troops, one of North Carolina, one of Virginia, and one of Maryland; Lieut. Col. Lee, with his Legion, covered our right flank; and Lieut. Col. [William] Henderson, with the State troops, our left. Lieut. Col. Washington, with his Cavalry and the Delaware troops, formed the body of reserve. Two three-pounders were in the front of our line, and two six-pounders with the second line. The Legion and the State troops formed our advanced guard, and were to retreat on our flanks when the enemy should form. We marched in this order to the attack.

The Legion and State troops met with a part of the enemy's horse and foot, about four miles from their camp, and put them to flight with fixed bayonets, having killed and wounded many. As we thought this was the van of the enemy, our first line was ordered to form, and the Legion and State troops to take post on our flanks. From this place of action to Eutaw Springs, the whole country is covered with wood. The firing began at three miles from the English camp. The militia advanced firing, and the advanced posts of the enemy were routed. The fire redoubled; our officers behaved with the greatest bravery, and the militia gained much honor by their firmness. But the fire of the enemy, who continued to advance, being superior to ours, the militia were obliged to retreat.

The Carolina Brigade, under Gen. [Jethro] Sumner, were ordered to support them, and, though not above three months raised, behaved nobly. In this moment of action, the Virginians, under Col. [Richard] Campbell, and the Marylanders, under Col. Williams, advanced in the face of the enemy's fire; a terrible cannonade, and a shower of bullets, overturned all that presented, and the enemy were put to the rout.

Lieut. Col. Lee turned his left flank to the enemy, and charged them in the rear, while the troops of Maryland and Virginia charged them in the front. Col. [Wade] Hampton, who commanded the troops of the State, charged on part, of whom he made one hundred prisoners. Col. Washington advanced with a corps de reserve upon the left, where the enemy appeared to prepare again to make resistance, and charged them so impetuously with his cavalry, and a body of infantry, that they had not time to rally.

We continued to pursue the enemy, after having broken them, until we attained their camp. A great number of prisoners fell into our hands, and some hundreds of fugitives escaped towards Charles Town; but a party having got into a brick house, three stories high, and others took post in a pallisadoed [palisaded] garden, their rear being covered by springs and hollow ways, the enemy renewed the fight. Lieut. Col. Washington did his utmost to dislodge them from a thick wood, but found it impossible; his horse was killed under him, and himself wounded, and taken prisoner. Four cannon were advanced against the house, but the fire from it was so brisk, that it was impossible to force it, or even to bring on the cannon, when the troops were ordered to retreat, and the greatest part of the officers and men who served those cannon were either killed or wounded.

Washington having failed in his attack on the left, the Legion could not succeed on the right; and seeing our foot [soldiers] roughly handled by the enemy's fire, and our ammunition almost expended, I thought it my duty to shelter them from the fire of the house, being persuaded that the enemy could maintain their posts but a few hours, and that we should have better play on their retreat, than to obstinately persist in dislodging them, which would expose us to a considerable loss.

We collected all our wounded, except those who were too forward under the fire of the house, and we returned to the bank, which we occupied in the morning, not finding water any where nearer, and our troops having great need of refreshment, after a fight which had continued four hours. I left upon the field of battle a strong picket.

I shall send Col. Lee and Gen. Marion early to-morrow morning between Eutaw and Charles Town, to prevent the reinforcements which may come to succor the enemy, or to retard their march, if they attempt to retreat, and give room to the army to attack their rear guard, and complete our success. We lost two pieces of artillery to the enemy, and we have taken one of theirs.

The night of the 9th the enemy retired, leaving more than seventy of their wounded behind them, and more than a thousand arms, which they had broken and concealed in the springs of the Eutaw's; they staved [broke] twenty or thirty barrels of rum, and destroyed a large quantity of provisions, which they could not carry with them.

We pursued them as soon as we had notice of their retreat, but they joined Major M'Arthur [Archibald McArthur], Gen. Marion and Col. Lee not having troops enough to hinder them. At our approach they retired to Charles Town. We took five hundred prisoners, including the wounded they had left behind; and I reckon they had not less than six hundred killed and wounded. The fugitives spread such an alarm that the enemy burnt their provisions at Dorchester, and quitted their post at Fair Lawn. A great number of negroes and others have been employed to throw down trees across the roads at some miles from Charles Town. Nothing but the brick house, and their strong post at Eutaw's, hindered the remains of the British army from falling into our hands.

We have pursued them to the Eutaw's, but could not overtake them. We shall rest here one or two days, and then take our old position near the heights of Santee.

I think I owe the victory which I have gained to the brisk use the Virginians and Marylanders, and one party of the infantry, made of the bayonet. I cannot forbear praising the conduct and courage of all my troops.

Nath. Greene

State of the Continental Troops

Killed: One Lieutenant Colonel, 6 Captains, 5 subalterns, 4 Sergeants, 98 rank and file. Wounded: Two

Lieutenant Colonels, 7 Captains, 20 Lieutenants, 24 Sergeants, 209 rank and file.

Total, 408 men.

NOTES

[1] R. W. Gibbes, *Documentary History of the American Revolution*, vol. 2 (Columbia, S.C.: Banner Steam-Power Press, 1853), 141–44.

[2] Michael Stephenson, *Patriot Battles: How the War of Independence Was Fought* (New York: Harper Perennial, 2008), 334.

A Loyalist Seeks Refuge

From *The Narrative of Colonel David Fanning*[1]

The British held on to Charleston for more than a year after Cornwallis surrendered at Yorktown. The back-country fighting between Whigs and Tories not only continued but in many ways grew more fierce. Once Britain's most able and aggressive field commander had given up, though, defeat was only a matter of time. Eventually, even the most die-hard loyalists saw what had to come.

For loyalists like David Fanning, the inevitable British withdrawal meant death. Even as Fanning resolved to leave behind his partisan days, the ascendant Whigs still sought him and his new bride. Fanning had to use all his wiles to elude and deceive the rebels until he, like hundreds of other Carolina Tories, could make his way to Charleston. Fanning and the other loyalist refugees first hoped to make a final stand against the Whigs, if only to force payment for the lands they would leave behind. When the British refused support for such a stand, though, the Tories gave up all they had in the Carolinas and sought transport for themselves and their families to the mother country or its other North American colonies.

Fanning left Charleston in November 1782, settling near the St. Johns River in Florida. When the British returned Florida to the Spanish in the Treaty of Paris, Fanning moved his family again, first to the Bahamas and then to Canada. He died in Nova Scotia in 1825.

The British evacuated Charleston in December 1782. The American Revolution in the Carolinas was over.

~

I concluded within myself, that it was better for me to try and settle myself, being weary of the disagreeable mode of living I had borne with for some considerable time. For the many kindness[es] and the civility of a gentleman who lived in the settlement of Deep River, I was induced to pay my addresses to his daughter, a young lady of sixteen years of age. The day of marriage being appointed; on making it known to my people, Capt. William Hooker, and Captain William Carr, agreed to be married with me. They both left me to make themselves and their intended wives ready. The day before we were to be coupled, the Rebels, before mentioned, with those good horses, attacked us[;] Cap't Hooker's horse being tied so fast he could not get him loose[,] they caught him and murdered him on the spot. Myself and Cap't Carr were married and kept two days merriment. The Rebels thought they were sure of me then; however, I took my wife and concealed her in the woods with Cap't Carr's, and caused an oration to be put out, that I was gone to Charleston. In order to be convinced, the Rebels sent a man in, as a spy, with two letters from [British] Gen'l [Alexander] Leslie with instructions for me to enlist men for the service which I knew was forged, in order to betray me, and from the person or Commanding Officer of the Rebel light horse. The following is one of which I gave Gen'l Leslie, that had his name signed to it.

Charlestown 20th Jan. 1782

Dear Colonel,

Altho I have not the happiness of being acquainted with you, yet I can applaud you very much, for your spirited con-duct and activity. The only objection I have to your conduct, is your being too strenuous with those who have been subjects to his Majesty, whom the Rebels have overcome and forced them to comply with their laws. If you would let them alone, the severity of the Rebels would cause them to return to their allegiance again. But Sir since you have made so brave a stand already, pray stand steadfast to the end, and we shall be well rewarded at the last. Try to spirit up your men, and enlist, if possible, three hundred men this spring, ready to join three hundred more, which shall be put under your command; and as many more as you can get, and you be Brigadier General of them. We shall, I hope, in the month of May land 1,300 troops in North Carolina, 300 of your corps, 1600 in the whole, to act upon the defensive, until you are reinforced.

Keep good discipline among your troops, and keep out fellows who will do nothing but plunder. They are but false dependents, and will not fight, but only corrupt good men. Every man you enlist for 12 months shall receive ten guineas; and a full suit of clothes; as soon as we land our troops, and they appear under your command ready for action. I can assure you, tis your fame and worthy actions has, through and by Major Craig given, reached his Majesty's ears, and I expect perhaps by the next packet boat you will get a genteel present from our gracious Sovereign. So hoping that you will be in the way of your duty, I will take leave of you, without mentioning your name, or subscribing mine, lest this might miscarry the man who is entrusted with the care of this. . . .

Sir yours

A letter from the traitor who brought these two letters from Gen'l Leslie:

Dear Sir

I would come to see you myself, but am afraid of the rebel light horse. I have a great many things to acquaint you with and a good deal of good news, but dare not write for fear of miscarriage. If you have any desire of seeing me you must come soon away, instantly. Don't let the bearer know the contents of the letters. The fewer trusted the better. In the mean time I am your friend and serv't.

April 29th, 1782

Joseph Wilson

My answer was in Major Rains's name as follows:

Sir,

I am very sorry to think that there is so many damned foolish Rebels in the world, as to think Col. Fanning would be ever deceived by such damned infernal writings, as I have received from you. Col. Fanning is gone to Charleston, and is not to return here till he comes with forces sufficient to defend this part of the country. I would have you to disband, and be gone immediately; for if I ever hear of any one of your people coming with any thing of the sort, I will come and kill them myself.

I am in behalf of his Majesty's armies

John Rains
Major of the Loyal Militia

I then proceeded to a Major Garner's truce land in Pee Dee in South Carolina, where I had made a truce with the Rebels, some time before; and I continued there until June, when I left my wife, horses, and negroes; as I was entirely a stranger to the situation of the country and roads, I was obliged to procure a pilot to proceed to Charleston; I could not get one for less than 20 guineas. After my departure I fell in with the rebel dragoons commanded by Col. Bailie, from Virginia. I was with them for about an hour, and informed them that we were some of the rebel party then on our way to General [Francis] Marion's head quarters. They never discovered otherwise; it being in the dusk of the evening. We fell into the rear, and went into the woods and struck our camp, and promised them we would see them next morning. However we proceeded on that night, and arrived at Herald's point on the 17th of June, and I immediately procured a passage to Charleston, when I immediately applied for a flag [of truce], to send after Mrs. Fanning and property. The flag had left Charleston two days, when she came in, as Maj. Gainey had applied to General Marion for a pass for her, to proceed to Charleston. He would not let her have any of our property, not even a negro to wait on her.

Soon after the Loyalists that had got to Charleston from different parts of the world hear[d] that the Southern Colonies were to be evacuated by the British forces, [they] called a meeting to point out some measures to try to hold some foothold in the country, until we had got some part payment for our property which we were obliged to leave if we ever left the country. Hand bills were printed and stuck up through out the town for the Loyalists to choose their representatives to represent our situation and the desire we had to support ourselves and property. It was proposed that 25 Gentlemen should be chosen [as] a committee for that purpose. The day was appointed to take the vote. I was chosen amongst others, and drew up a petition and sent to Sir Guy Carleton, Commander in Chief, praying the liberty of keeping the town and artillery, as they then stood on the works; and dispatched two gentlemen off with our petition. Our request was not granted.

NOTES

[1]David Fanning, *The Narrative of Colonel David Fanning, A Tory in the Revolutionary War with Great Britain* (New York: reprinted for Joseph Sabin, 1865), 56–61.

Bibliography

PRIMARY SOURCES

Collins, James Potter. *Autobiography of a Revolutionary Soldier*. Revised and prepared by John M. Roberts. Clinton, La.: *Feliciana Democrat*, 1859.

Draper, Lyman C. *King's Mountain and Its Heroes: History of the Battle of King's Mountain, October 7th, 1780, and the Events Which Led to It*. Cincinnati, Ohio: Peter G. Thomson, Publisher, 1881.

Fanning, David. *The Narrative of Colonel David Fanning, A Tory in the Revolutionary War with Great Britain*. New York: reprinted for Joseph Sabin, 1865.

Gibbes, R. W. *Documentary History of the American Revolution*. Vol. 1. New York: D. Appleton & Co., 1855.

———. *Documentary History of the American Revolution*. Vol. 2. Columbia, S.C.: Banner Steam-Power Press, 1853.

———. *Documentary History of the American Revolution*. Vol. 3. New York: D. Appleton & Co., 1857.

Graham, James. *The Life of General Daniel Morgan, of the Virginia Line of the Army of the United States, with Portions of His Correspondence*. New York: Derby & Jackson, 1856.

Graham, William A. *General Joseph Graham and His Papers on North Carolina Revolutionary History*. Raleigh, N.C.: Edwards & Broughton, 1904.

Henry, Robert. *Narrative of the Battle of Cowan's Ford, February 1st, 1781*. Greensboro, N.C.: D. Schenck, Sr., 1891.

Hill, William. *Colonel William Hill's Memoirs of the Revolution*. Columbia: Historical Commission of South Carolina, 1921.

Horry, Peter, and M. L. Weems. *The Life of General Francis Marion.* Winston-Salem, N.C.: John F. Blair, Publisher, 2000.

Johnson, William. *Sketches of the Life and Correspondence of Nathanael Greene, Major General of the Armies of the United States, in the War of the Revolution.* Vol. 1. Charleston, S.C.: A. E. Miller, 1822.

Lee, Henry. *Memoirs of the War in the Southern Department of the United States.* New York: University Publishing Company, 1870.

Moultrie, William. *Memoirs of the American Revolution, So Far As It Related to the States of North and South-Carolina, and Georgia.* Vol. 2. New York: David Longworth, 1802.

Robinson, Blackwell P., ed. *The Revolutionary War Sketches of William R. Davie.* Raleigh: North Carolina Department of Cultural Resources, Division of Archives and History, 1976.

Tarleton, Banastre. *A History of the Campaigns of 1780 and 1781 in the Southern Provinces of North America.* Dublin: printed for Colles, Exshaw, White, H. Whitestone, Burton, etc., 1787.

Young, Thomas. *The Memoir of Major Thomas Young.* Penfield, Ga.: *Orion* magazine, 1843.

SECONDARY SOURCES

Barefoot, Daniel W. *Touring North Carolina's Revolutionary War Sites.* Winston-Salem, N.C.: John F. Blair, Publisher, 1998.

———. *Touring South Carolina's Revolutionary War Sites.* Winston-Salem, N.C.: John F. Blair, Publisher, 1999.

Billias, George Athan, ed. *George Washington's Generals.* New York: William Morrow and Company, 1964.

Brands, H. W. *Andrew Jackson: His Life and Times.* New York: Doubleday, 2005.

Buchanan, John. *Jackson's Way: Andrew Jackson and the People of the Western Waters.* New York: John Wiley & Sons, 2001.

————. *The Road to Guilford Courthouse: The American Revolution in the Carolinas*. New York: John Wiley & Sons, 1997.

Cox, Caroline. *A Proper Sense of Honor: Service and Sacrifice in George Washington's Army*. Chapel Hill: University of North Carolina Press, 2004.

Davis, Burke. *The Cowpens–Guilford Courthouse Campaign*. 1962. Reprint, Philadelphia: University of Pennsylvania Press, 2003.

Edgar, Walter. *Partisans and Redcoats: The Southern Conflict That Turned the Tide of the American Revolution*. New York: Harper Perennial, 2003.

Fischer, David Hackett. *Albion's Seed: Four British Folkways in America*. New York: Oxford University Press, 1989.

Fulghum, R. Neil. *William Richardson Davie: Soldier, Statesman, and Founder of the University of North Carolina*. Chapel Hill: University of North Carolina, 2006. This booklet was published to complement the 2006 William Richardson Davie exhibition in the North Carolina Collection gallery at the Wilson Library.

Hairr, John. *Guilford Courthouse: Nathanael Greene's Victory in Defeat, March 15, 1781*. Cambridge, Mass.: DaCapo Press, 2002.

McNitt, V. V. *Chain of Error and the Mecklenburg Declaration of Independence*. Charlotte, N.C.: Mecklenburg Historical Association, 1996.

Pancake, John S. *This Destructive War: The British Campaign in the Carolinas, 1780–1782*. Tuscaloosa: University of Alabama Press, 1985.

Powell, William S. *North Carolina: A History*. Chapel Hill: University of North Carolina Press, 1988.

Stephenson, Michael. *Patriot Battles: How the War of Independence Was Fought*. New York: Harper Perennial, 2008.

Tuchman, Barbara. *The First Salute: A View of the American Revolution*. New York: Ballantine Books, 1989.

Wood, W. J. *Battles of the Revolutionary War, 1775–1781*. Chapel Hill, N.C.: Algonquin Books of Chapel Hill, 1990.